Sommer

Nachi Sklar

Page 51

A Celebration of Poets

East
Grades K-3
Fall 2010

A Celebration of Poets
East
Grades K-3
Fall 2010

An anthology compiled by Creative Communication, Inc.

Published by:

1488 NORTH 200 WEST • LOGAN, UTAH 84341
TEL. 435-713-4411 • WWW.POETICPOWER.COM

All rights reserved. No part of this book may be reproduced or transmitted in any form or by any means, electronic or mechanical without written permission of the author and publisher.

Copyright © 2011 by Creative Communication, Inc.
Printed in the United States of America

ISBN: 978-1-60050-406-8

FOREWORD

As we start our nineteenth year of working with student writers across the US and Canada, I think back on the positive effects created by our contests and anthologies. Each year I receive hundreds of letters from students who state that being accepted to be published created a spark that brightened their educational experience. Years later, after these students have graduated, I have other letters that report back on successes after high school. These letters are from students who credited Creative Communication as the start of their writing career and have now published their first book of poems or a novel.

These letters help us to know the importance of what we do. I always tell our judges that behind the entries are students whose lives can be changed. I tell them that Creative Communication doesn't publish poems and essays, we publish hopes and dreams.

So here we are, another contest completed and more "hopes and dreams" being published. We hope that these entries fulfill their purpose of entertaining you and helping these student authors know that they have met a milestone in their lives. The poems in this book represent the best and brightest of today's student writers. Enjoy, and realize that the Hemmingways, Plaths or Frosts of tomorrow may be published today, between these pages.

Sincerely,

Thomas Worthen, Ph.D.
Editor
Creative Communication

WRITING CONTESTS!

Enter our next POETRY contest!
Enter our next ESSAY contest!

Why should I enter?
Win prizes and get published! Each year thousands of dollars in prizes are awarded throughout North America. The top writers in each division receive a monetary award and a free book that includes their published poem or essay. Entries of merit are also selected to be published in our anthology.

Who may enter?
There are four divisions in the poetry contest. The poetry divisions are grades K-3, 4-6, 7-9, and 10-12. There are three divisions in the essay contest. The essay divisions are grades 3-6, 7-9, and 10-12.

What is needed to enter the contest?
To enter the poetry contest send in one original poem, 21 lines or less. To enter the essay contest send in one original non-fiction essay, 250 words or less, on any topic. Each entry must include the student's name, grade, address, city, state, and zip code, and the student's school name and school address. Students who include their teacher's name may help their teacher qualify for a free copy of the anthology. Contest changes and updates are listed at www.poeticpower.com.

How do I enter?
Enter a poem online at:
www.poeticpower.com
or
Mail your poem to:
  Poetry Contest
  1488 North 200 West
  Logan, UT 84341

Enter an essay online at:
www.poeticpower.com
or
Mail your essay to:
  Essay Contest
  1488 North 200 West
  Logan, UT 84341

When is the deadline?
Poetry contest deadlines are August 16th, December 6th, and April 5th. Essay contest deadlines are July 19th, October 18th, and February 15th. Students can enter one poem and one essay for each spring, summer, and fall contest deadline.

Are there benefits for my school?
Yes. We award $12,500 each year in grants to help with Language Arts programs. Schools qualify to apply for a grant by having 15 or more accepted entries.

Are there benefits for my teacher?
Yes. Teachers with five or more students published receive a free anthology that includes their students' writing.

For more information please go to our website at
www.poeticpower.com,
email us at editor@poeticpower.com or call 435-713-4411.

Table of Contents

Poetic Achievement Honor Schools   1

Language Arts Grant Recipients   7

Grades K-1-2-3 High Merit Poems 11

Index 153

STATES INCLUDED IN THIS EDITION:

CONNECTICUT
DELAWARE
DISTRICT OF COLUMBIA
FLORIDA
MAINE
MARYLAND
MASSACHUSETTS
NEW HAMPSHIRE
NEW JERSEY
NEW YORK
PENNSYLVANIA
RHODE ISLAND
VERMONT
VIRGINIA

Fall 2010 Poetic Achievement Honor Schools

* Teachers who had fifteen or more poets accepted to be published

The following schools are recognized as receiving a "Poetic Achievement Award." This award is given to schools who have a large number of entries of which over fifty percent are accepted for publication. With hundreds of schools entering our contest, only a small percent of these schools are honored with this award. The purpose of this award is to recognize schools with excellent Language Arts programs. This award qualifies these schools to receive a complimentary copy of this anthology. In addition, these schools are eligible to apply for a Creative Communication Language Arts Grant. Grants of two hundred and fifty dollars each are awarded to further develop writing in our schools.

Bensley Elementary School
Richmond, VA
  Carolyn Booth
  Amanda Collins
  Christy Frear
  Katie Griffin
  Maria T. MacLaughlin*
  Satonya Perry

Blessed Sacrament School
Seminole, FL
  Linda Susens*

Carlyle C Ring Elementary School
Jamestown, NY
  Marcella Centi*

Central Park Elementary School
Plantation, FL
  Kristen Marsolek
  Mark Siegel*

Clover Street School
Windsor, CT
  Lisa Thomas*

Consolidated School
New Fairfield, CT
  Amy Johnson*

Fairview Elementary School
Midland, PA
  Donna Harn*
  Rose Onuska*

A Celebration of Poets – East Grades K-3 Fall 2010

Infant Jesus School
Nashua, NH
  Elaine Hebert*

Interboro GATE Program
Prospect Park, PA
  Sandi D'Alessandro*
  Joyce Faragasso*

Jeffrey Elementary School
Madison, CT
  Ella Cinquino
  Esther R. Magee

Kane Area Elementary/Middle School
Kane, PA
  Robynn Boyer*

Marie Curie Institute
Amsterdam, NY
  Jerilynn Einarsson*
  Diana L. Giardino*
  Jennifer Satas*
  Linda Sawicki*

Mary Walter Elementary School
Bealeton, VA
  Patricia Baker*

McKinley Elementary School
Elkins Park, PA
  Dennis Donnelly
  Linda Hagarty
  Mrs. Hazelwood*
  Ms. Kelly
  Tricia Livingood*
  Marsha Marcy*
  Julia McGettigan

McKinley Elementary School (cont.)
Elkins Park, PA
  Deepika McGinley*
  Miss Murphy
  Mr. Pinkashov
  Joanne Stoll
  Mr. West

Memorial School
Bedford, NH
  Courtney Hannah*

Mother Seton Inter Parochial School
Union City, NJ
  Karla Giron
  Marisol Rodriguez
  Karen Shkop
  Miss Smith
  Miss Tobin

New York Institute for Special Education
Bronx, NY
  Lillian M. Ludwig
  Dr. Franklin D. Raddock*

Northeast Elementary School
Brentwood, NY
  Mrs. Correa
  Lisa Patrick*
  Andrea Pugliese*

Oak Ridge Elementary School
Harleysville, PA
  Ross Pollack*

Poetic Achievement Honor Schools

Our Lady of Hope School
Middle Village, NY
  Martha Madri*
  Ellie McAuley

Our Lady of Mercy Regional School
Cutchogue, NY
  Alicia Hunt
  Miss McGoey
  Nicole Salvo
  AnnaMarie Spina
  Mrs. Wachtel
  Jennifer Wagner

Public School 131
Brooklyn, NY
  Elizabeth Acevedo
  Anita Betances*

Public School 85 Charles Vallone
Astoria, NY
  Ms. D'Angelo
  Mr. Douros
  Mrs. Kamarinos
  Mrs. Koh
  Mrs. Laris
  Ms. Najeddine
  Ellen Schild
  Mrs. West

Richard E Byrd Elementary School
Glen Rock, NJ
  Cindy Lota
  Andrea Mayernik
  Viola Stanley

Ross Elementary School
Pittsburgh, PA
  Maddy Gillingham
  Karen Jones*

St Agatha School
Brooklyn, NY
  Rosemarie Paredes*

St Alexis School
Wexford, PA
  Sandra Ross*

St Augustine Cathedral School
Bridgeport, CT
  Susan Gulyas*
  Mrs. Volpe

St James School
Basking Ridge, NJ
  Katherine Morra*

St John the Apostle Catholic School
Virginia Beach, VA
  Katie Gieselman
  Elise Normile

St Mary School
East Islip, NY
  Nicole Barattini*

St Mary's School
Pompton Lakes, NJ
  Patricia Andrews*
  Elizabeth Green*
  Edie Kimak*
  Kateryna Kucyna*
  Carol Porada*

A Celebration of Poets – East Grades K-3 Fall 2010

St Stephen's School
Grand Island, NY
Kristy Pasko*
Daniela Schmidt*

Susquehanna Community
Elementary School
Susquehanna, PA
Dawn Steele*

Sweetwater Episcopal Academy
Longwood, FL
Pam Wolfcale*

The American Academy
Philadelphia, PA
Dr. Sharon Traver*

Triangle Elementary School
Hillsborough, NJ
Kim Menchu*
Mrs. Verano*

Virginia A Boone Highland
Oaks Elementary School
North Miami Beach, FL
Phillis Diskin
Stephanie Sheir
Mrs. Sweetman

Wanamassa Elementary School
Wanamassa, NJ
Carin Francisco
Deborah Kiss*
Kathleen Marmora

Wapping Elementary School
South Windsor, CT
Karrieann Noble*

Weston Elementary School
Manville, NJ
Laura Landau*

William M Meredith School
Philadelphia, PA
Elizabeth Cieri*
Deborah Coy
Robert Hamm*
Joyce Kemmler
Tamarah Rash
Kelly Schaaf*
Maisha
 Williams-Bradley

Windsor Learning Academy
Tampa, FL
Amy Ayres*
Miss Brenda
Tammy Cornelius
Miss Lisset
Miss Melissa

Worthington Hooker School –
K-2 Campus
New Haven, CT
Kathy Lembo*

Yeshiva Ketana of Long Island
Inwood, NY
Mrs. Kelemer*

Language Arts Grant Recipients 2010-2011

After receiving a "Poetic Achievement Award" schools are encouraged to apply for a Creative Communication Language Arts Grant. The following is a list of schools who received a two hundred and fifty dollar grant for the 2010-2011 school year.

Arrowhead Union High School, Hartland, WI
Adolph Schreiber Hebrew Academy, Monsey, NY
August Boeger Middle School, San Jose, CA
Bedford Road School, Pleasantville, NY
Benton Central Jr/Sr High School, Oxford, IN
Birchwood School, Cleveland, OH
Blue Ball Elementary School, Blue Ball, PA
Bonneville High School, Idaho Falls, ID
Cedar Ridge High School, Newark, AR
Corpus Christi School, San Francisco, CA
Crestwood Elementary School, Rockford, MI
Dodson Elementary School, Canton, MI
Dr Howard K Conley Elementary School, Chandler, AZ
Eastport Elementary School, Eastport, ME
Emmanuel-St Michael Lutheran School, Fort Wayne, IN
Fannin County Middle School, Blue Ridge, GA
Fort Recovery Elementary School, Fort Recovery, OH
Frank Ohl Intermediate School, Youngstown, OH
Frenship Middle School, Wolfforth, TX
Gateway Pointe Elementary School, Gilbert, AZ
Greencastle-Antrim Middle School, Greencastle, PA
Greenville High School, Greenville, AL
Hancock County High School, Sneedville, TN

Language Arts Grant Winners cont.

Holy Child Academy, Drexel Hill, PA
Holy Cross High School, Delran, NJ
Holy Family Catholic School, Granite City, IL
Interboro GATE Program, Prospect Park, PA
John E Riley Elementary School, South Plainfield, NJ
Joseph M Simas Elementary School, Hanford, CA
Lee A Tolbert Community Academy, Kansas City, MO
Malvern Middle School, Malvern, OH
Merritt Central Elementary School, Merritt, BC
Metcalf School, Exeter, RI
Norfolk Christian Middle School, Norfolk, VA
Pioneer Career & Technology Center, Shelby, OH
Providence Hall, Herriman, UT
Ramsay School, Ramsay, MT
Reuben Johnson Elementary School, McKinney, TX
Round Lake High School, Round Lake, MN
Sacred Heart School, Oxford, PA
Selwyn College Preparatory School, Denton, TX
Shadowlawn Elementary School, Green Cove Springs, FL
St Elizabeth Catholic School, Rockville, MD
St Lorenz Lutheran School, Frankenmuth, MI
The Oakridge School, Arlington, TX
Tomlin Middle School, Plant City, FL
Vista Fundamental School, Simi Valley, CA
Walsh Elementary School, Walsh, CO
Washington County Union School, Roper, NC
Woodland Intermediate School, Gurnee, IL
Woodward Granger High School, Woodward, IA

Grades K-1-2-3 Top Ten Winners

List of Top Ten Winners for Grades K-3; listed alphabetically

Adit Agarwal, Grade 3
Oak Hill Elementary School, KS

Oliver Chen, Grade 3
Fellows Elementary School, IA

Abigail Gruner, Grade 2
Crest Hill Elementary School, WY

Alex Hall, Grade 3
Love Memorial Elementary School, NC

Ryan Harvey, Grade 3
La Mariposa Montessori School, NM

Malone Krouch, Grade 3
Jeffrey Elementary School, CT

Dysan McCray, Grade 1
Arnold Elementary School, GA

Laura Null, Grade 3
The American Academy, PA

Alyson Smith, Grade 3
Sherwood Public School, ON

Kyle Woodruff, Grade 3
Crest Hill Elementary School, WY

All Top Ten Poems can be read at www.poeticpower.com

Note: The Top Ten poems were finalized through an online voting system. Creative Communication's judges first picked out the top poems. These poems were then posted online. The final step involved thousands of students and teachers who registered as the online judges and voted for the Top Ten poems. We hope you enjoy these selections.

A Celebration of Poets – East Grades K-3 Fall 2010

My Frightening Nightmare

Once when I fell into a deep sleep I dreamed I had fallen into a pit
And when I had landed I had made a split.

I yelled and yelled for help, but no one came.
I got so angry I almost burst into a flame.

So, I set up a trap to try to catch food.
But, instead, I got nothing which put me in a bad mood.

That night I slept on the ground and I had no night shirt!
Sleeping in a hot desert, it really hurt!

As the long hot days passed, food began to sprinkle by.
But with no water in sight, I thought I would die!

When winter came, it was dry and chilly.
And because there was no snow I laughed myself silly.

When spring came I was sad to say I couldn't live, I died!
But with the air being so dry, I was mummified!

When I woke up, I thought I was laying in a deep dark pit.
Then I realized I was in my room, because a candle was lit.

Caroline Fischer, Grade 3
Infant Jesus School, NH

Goodbye November, Hello December!

November is the month of fall,
Thanksgiving treats and fun for all.
December is the month of snow,
Santa Claus comes and Santa Claus goes.

November is the month of trees,
smell the fragrance of the crisp, clean breeze.
December is the month of gloves,
hear the song of the turtledoves.

Goodbye November and hello December,
the months are starting to run.
So put on your jackets and put on your boots,
And get ready to have some fun!

Prasanna Krishnamoorthy, Grade 3
Robert S. Gallaher Elementary School, DE

High Merit Poems – Grades K, 1, 2, and 3

The Times I Love My Mom

I love my mother, my mom.
She hugs me and kisses me.
She cooks such good food, sandwiches and omelets.

She makes me feel so good.
So, I feel lots and lots of love for her.
I try to be nice to her by being good.

I'm glad she's in my life; because
love is good.
She plays with me — lots of games and Legos.

That's my mom.

Jayden Ferriera, Grade 3
New York Institute for Special Education, NY

Tiger

Never does it make a sound,
To sneak up on its prey,
Orange, black, orange, black,
Claws are coming out,
Ready to attack,
Orange, black, orange, black,
It takes its prey into its den,
Never to be seen again.

You may think tigers are a violent creature,
But as I learned from my teacher,
Tigers are gentle as can be,
And they are as loving as you and me.

Alyson Brown, Grade 3
Memorial School, NH

My Life as a Wampanoag Girl

I live in Massachusetts near the bay or near a small lake.
I sleep in a wetu and inside my wetu are animal skins for my blankets and a smoke hole.
During the summer, the Wampanoag lived in cleared areas where they could plant corn.
Both men and women wore jewelry which was crafted from stone, bone, and wampum clam.

Justina Figueroa, Grade 3
St Mary School, NY

Twisters

It touches down.
A breeze whips around me.

Clouds turn black.
More touches down,
and tosses up debris.

Wind is soaring madly around me.
The wind whispers to me, and blows back my hair.

It runs away from me.
The wind gets calm.

I call them twisters.

Evan Wightman, Grade 3
Oak Ridge Elementary School, PA

My Super Best Friend

My best friend forever is someone who cares about me.
Together we share secrets and important things.
I care about her and she cares about me.
She is not jealous of me and I am not jealous of her.

Whenever I go to class, I see her smiling at me.
We play and talk together.
Her name is Amena Begum.
It doesn't matter that the color of her skin is different from mine,
she has a gentle heart.
We have different opinions but we respect and love each other.
We will always be the super best friends to the end.
We are members of TMK (The Magical Kids).
We are two special best friends.

Jiaming Liu, Grade 3
Public School 131, NY

Pumpkin Fighter

Pumpkin, pumpkin fighting in the ring.
Wearing your mask and goggles strapped with a string.
When you come out, with seeds on your teeth,
You take off your mask and say "My name is Keith!
The Pumpkin Fighter."

Damon Bloom, Grade 3
Coral Springs Elementary School, FL

High Merit Poems – Grades K, 1, 2, and 3

The Rat and the Cat

Once there was a cat and a rat that were very, very fat.
Then one day they decided to play and the cat wore his funny hat.
The cat's name was Taylor and the rat's name was Bill.
Taylor and Bill played up on the hill.
In the night they could see really far.
During the night, they could see a really big star.
There they would make a very fine wish.
It would be to always have food on their dish.
Taylor and Bill went back to the hill.
They got their wish, a dish full of fish!
They got their wish and what do you think?
They both got as big as a kitchen sink!

Jordyn Sherry, Grade 2
Infant Jesus School, NH

Moon

The moon stretches.
The earth gets darker and darker.
Beads of the moon shine.
I hear the moon peeping a thousand whispers to the shining stars.
Wind streams silently.
Pebbles on the moon are resting in peace.
Ice stones pass the whispers,
And wonder what the moon is saying.
A texture of black sky,
As dark as an eclipse surrounding the moon.
The whistles of the moon whisper in my ear.
It sends warm dreams to my heart.

Shannon Hollick, Grade 3
Oak Ridge Elementary School, PA

The Lion Who Lies

Never sit beside a lion cause he might be lying
Then you're going to be crying
You went to the monkey
But he was too funky

You went to bake a cake
But the lion said he was going to throw it in the lake
Then I made another cake but it came out lame
Then the lion said it should be on the hall of fame

Kaylah Langley, Grade 3
Bensley Elementary School, VA

My Two Sisters

I have two sisters one is two, one is three
We don't always get along
Because they are younger than me
But sisters are great
It's like having two best friends
Even though sometimes they are annoying
They are my sisters
And I'll love them 'til the end!

Madison Serttas, Grade 3
Mary Walter Elementary School, VA

Terrance

Funny, Silly, Happy,
Son of Stephanie and Bill
Loves hockey, dogs, cats,
Who likes pizza, bread, corn
Who hates fast rides, PB&J
Who would like to ride dirt bikes, race boats, race bikes
Resident of Grand Island
Oehler

Terrance Oehler, Grade 2
St Stephen's School, NY

Teachers

T eachers are the best
E ating healthy foods make teachers strong
A t school I have the best teacher
C lassrooms are where we learn
H igh grades are what teachers like
E very day is a challenge
R eading books to the class
S aying goodbye in June

Cynthia Flores, Grade 3
Bensley Elementary School, VA

I Love Autumn

Leaves change into different colors like red, green, and yellow,
We smell pumpkin pie that smells so, so good and tasty,
We can hear the leaves falling from the trees on a windy day,
What a wonderful taste of apple pie, Mmmmm, it is very, very good!
When I rake the leaves, I like to make piles and jump in them after!

Isabella Dreyer, Grade 2
Wellington School, FL

Lightning

When lightning comes, some people scream
like animals attacking them.
Some people wish they could go outside
if it were not pouring lightning.

Some people think that lightning should
be in a horror movie.
Some people think that lightning
should be in a humor movie.

The lightning gets stronger and tougher.

Some people put their scary face on.
Some people put their happy face on.

But then they go outside and they get shocked.
The lightning caught them.

Light came on their body.
They got shocked by THUNDER.

Cindy Rodriguez Garcia, Grade 3
Oak Ridge Elementary School, PA

Coral Reef

As a shark glides through the water
All silver, blue, and white.
Fish like multi-colored shirts.
The coral oh so like trees.
Snail's shells gleaming in the silver waves.
And a whale big as a giant!
As a lobster trudged through the dangers of the sea
Unaware of a carpet shark waiting silently like a rock.
As a diver jumps in,
a school of fish swim by like a strong gust of wind.
A parrot fish starts to snack!
The cleaners clean fish
And get lots of food
As a moray pops his head out
As night falls.
And the sea of sleep begins!

Leo Rupp-Coppi, Grade 3
Jeffrey Elementary School, CT

A Celebration of Poets – East Grades K-3 Fall 2010

What I Found in My Closet*
A beautiful yellow flower,
A broken Lego tower,
A very shiny nickel,
An icky sticky pickle,
My cute missing kitten,
My very old mitten,
My toy Christmas tree,
A picture of me,
A Magic Tree House book,
A sharp and broken hook,
And one more thing I must confess,
A note from Mother: "Clean up this mess!"

Lexi Welton, Grade 2
Blessed Sacrament School, FL
**Patterned after "What I Found in My Desk" by Bruce Lansky*

What I Found in My Dresser*
A bug that was leaping,
A chick that was peeping,
A note from my friend Pete,
A chicken leg I did not eat,
A bald set of dice,
A bowl of fried rice,
An old pair of sneakers,
Two broken down speakers,
A worn out dog collar,
My long-lost gold dollar,
And one more thing I must confess,
A note from Dad: "Clean up this mess!"

Michael Gomes, Grade 2
Blessed Sacrament School, FL
**Patterned after "What I Found in My Desk" by Bruce Lansky*

White
Bunnies are white.
Snowflakes are white too.
White is so famous!
Ghost are white and not blue.
If you drive through snow, your car will be white.
White is the best color.
It is out of sight.

Daniel Frew, Grade 2
Sweetwater Episcopal Academy, FL

In Winter

In winter when the snowflakes fall the loud wind starts to call.
The shivering icicles on the tree, I hope one doesn't fall on me!
Most of the trees are bare and there's so many things I have to wear.
I sled down a tall mountain too and if I'm still cold I build an igloo.
I make a snow angel and a snowflake too.
I love winter and I hope you do too!

Quinn Klessel, Grade 3
Shady Grove Elementary School, PA

Autumn

A ll the leaves are falling
U se your sweater in autumn
T oast will be at the feast
U se an umbrella and watch out for the leaves
M ake turkey please
N obody can resist mashed potatoes

Carlos Galan, Grade 3
Central Park Elementary School, FL

Winter

W inter time winter time having fun at winter time,
I n the snow making snowball from the ground,
N o one is hot everybody is chilling inside,
T iny tiny icicles on the roof like backwards cones,
E very day kids having fun in the snow,
R aining snowflakes to the ground.

Carly Amato, Grade 3
Shady Grove Elementary School, PA

Cold Winter Day

The winter is really cold,
The wind is blowing.
Winter is fun,
Because the trees are flowing.

Daniel Broides, Grade 2
Virginia A Boone Highland Oaks Elementary School, FL

The Seasons

Fall is warm and the leaves turn colors.
Summer is hot; you want to go in the pool.
Winter is cold, and Santa comes!

Christopher Santos, Grade 2
Sweetwater Episcopal Academy, FL

Courtney
Courtney
Pretty and smart
Sibling of Allison
Lover of chocolate and playing soccer
Who fears thunderstorms and heights
Who would like to see Ireland and the Caribbean
Resident of Rockledge, PA
Kehoe

Courtney Kehoe, Grade 3
McKinley Elementary School, PA

Anna
Anna
Caring and playful
Sibling of Grace Kirwin
Lover of owls and reading
Who fears being alone and falling off my bike
Who would like to see the real Santa and a forest
Resident of Elkins Park, PA
Kirwin

Anna Kirwin, Grade 3
McKinley Elementary School, PA

Jake
Jake
Silly and nudgey
Sibling of Mia
Lover of Legos and drawing
Who fears snakes and bears
Who would like to see a Yankees game and the Lego factory
Resident of Jenkintown, PA
Zucker

Jacob Zucker, Grade 3
McKinley Elementary School, PA

Legos
Legos are fun and all so cool…
you can make a city and come up with a rule.
NO ONE CAN COME IN!
Be the king and make a store for people to come by…
and a lego home for friends to visit.

Jack Rizzo, Grade 2
St John the Apostle Catholic School, VA

Ode to Sun
Oh Sun,
You're a giant super star
In the middle of our system.
You rise each and every day
And you shine, shine, shine!

David Rodriguez, Grade 2
Worthington Hooker School – K-2 Campus, CT

The Love I Have for My Family
I love my family.
They're always there when I'm mad.
I am super lucky to have my family.
I show them how much I love them
   by telling them every day.
I will always love them!

Anthony Alverio, Grade 3
New York Institute for Special Education, NY

My Family
My family is good to me
as you will see
We go to the park
We play games and basketball until it gets dark
We have so much fun hanging out
It makes me want to shout

A'Mair Buffaloe, Grade 3
Number 12 Elementary School, NJ

Winter
Winter is cold,
It makes my teeth chatter.
I do not like winter that much,
But that does not matter!

Abigail Plewinski, Grade 2
Virginia A Boone Highland Oaks Elementary School, FL

Winter
Cold winter day I really want to play.
I grab my coat and boots.
I see my friends and now we can finally play.

Alexandra Buonanno, Grade 2
St Mary's School, NJ

A Celebration of Poets – East Grades K-3 Fall 2010

Coconuts
They are full of milk
They are a little heavy
Hiding on Palm trees
Zev Braunschweig, Grade 3
Yeshiva Ketana of Long Island, NY

Coconuts
I love coconuts
they are yummy and fuzzy
they are round and brown
Chaim Laundau, Grade 3
Yeshiva Ketana of Long Island, NY

Summer Day
A hot summer day!
Swimming in my backyard pool,
I love the hot summer days!
Olivia Vallo, Grade 2
St Mary's School, NJ

Beaches
Beaches are sandy
salty water burns my eyes
it never dries up
Chaim Bugayer, Grade 3
Yeshiva Ketana of Long Island, NY

A Lion
It's very hairy
They catch their pray by running
King of the Jungle
Aaron Mindell, Grade 3
Yeshiva Ketana of Long Island, NY

Red
Red is the color for a ball.
Red is the color for an apple.
Red is the color for a tomato.
Cameron Caggiano, Grade 2
Sweetwater Episcopal Academy, FL

Rockets Up High
Rockets are the best I've seen
When the rockets are off the ground
They're seen as small as beans.
Yongjae Nam, Grade 2
Corl Street Elementary School, PA

My Birthday
My Birthday is soon
It's at Twisters, my Birthday
It's gonna be fun
Ivy Koreyva, Grade 3
Walnut Street Elementary School, NJ

Storm
It rains cats and dogs
There is a lot of puddles
Then the sun comes out
Ephraim Schreck, Grade 3
Yeshiva Ketana of Long Island, NY

Shark
They swim in the sea
They eat fish really quickly
They have sharp teeth.
David Wolberg, Grade 3
Yeshiva Ketana of Long Island, NY

Football
Football's amazing.
It smells bad like wet grass, smash.
I love the Giants.
Jacob Dawson, Grade 3
Walnut Street Elementary School, NJ

Beaches
Beaches are so fun
swim in the salty ocean
playing in the sand.
David Gordon, Grade 3
Yeshiva Ketana of Long Island, NY

High Merit Poems – Grades K, 1, 2, and 3

My Brother

My brother is fussy (sometimes) and cute
he loves to play his electric guitar
he'll put on a dress
and dance around
he runs around crazy having fun!
until he

falls

down.
May Goar, Grade 3
Thoreau Elementary School, MA

The Sun and How Hot Places Are

If you never played in the sun,
try it and it might be fun.
Florida is very hot,
but it's my favorite spot.
In America you can't freeze,
but in the North Pole you sure can, jeeze!
In the South Pole the temperature is low,
and in some places rivers flow.
Some people think the sun is lame,
but the sun is a very important flame!
Sam Berchtold, Grade 3
Ellicott Road Elementary School, NY

Roma

Roma is my pet,
and she likes to go to the vet.
She is a little dog,
and she eats like a hog.
Roma likes me to rub her belly,
but she is very smelly.
She likes to play in the sun,
and it looks like a lot of fun.
Roma likes to run and play,
and she does it all day!
Abby Bell, Grade 3
Ellicott Road Elementary School, NY

Peace Is...

Loving each other,
A heart full of love,
Quiet like a baby,
Looking at a rainbow,
The bright orange sun,
Birds chirping,
Dreaming about a cloud raining,
Caring for people,
But most of all,
Peace is sleeping and being quiet.
Vida Harris, Grade 3
St Augustine Cathedral School, CT

Hockey

I like hockey a lot,
because you get to take shots.
I don't like getting dressed,
but I think it is best.
The zamboni cleans the ice,
after it gets sliced.
You should always pass,
It will get the puck moving fast.
I was coming in on goal,
And I hit the pole.
Mike Naples, Grade 3
Ellicott Road Elementary School, NY

Peace Is...

Loving your mom.
Calm by watching a movie.
Reading a Magic Tree House book.
Relaxing on a bed.
Caring for my mom.
Sleeping on a comfy bed.
A waterfall.
Birds chirping in the morning.
But most of all,
Peace is loving my mom very much.
Marcos Ardila, Grade 3
St Augustine Cathedral School, CT

Our Night

We drift along the silent
sea as the waves sing to
us the waves as blue, blue like
it is borrowed from the sky.
How bright is the moon tonight?
The waves as swift as snow being as gentle as
A whale
The secrets
Of the dark
Dancing far
Below as the silver sea wraps in its loving arms
It cradles us in our cozy boat
Drift us to sleep
Drift us to sleep
Good night!

Karen Newton, Grade 3
Jeffrey Elementary School, CT

My Mom Takes Care of Me

I love my mommy a lot
She takes care of me and feeds me
She cooks oatmeal for me
I feel sad when I think about my mother because
I miss her so much
I am a residential student and only see her on the weekends
I like this school but not being residential

I behave at home to show my mom I love her
I take care of my baby brother and
Listen and respect my older brothers
My mom is the most important thing to me because
She's my mommy
She takes my brothers and me to the park

Daryel Correa, Grade 3
New York Institute for Special Education, NY

Horse

My horse walks on the sidewalk
Clippity clop, clippity clop
My horse walks on.
Its tail sways in the wind; sways in the wind.

Maya Malishewsky, Grade 2
Sweetwater Episcopal Academy, FL

Werewolf

W here the werewolves hide in the dark, windy, spooky cave at the
E nd of the creepy forest. They
R oam through the cold, slimy cave.
E very night the werewolves beady eyes are glowing in the misty forest.
W olves are turning into werewolves. All creepy, ugly, spooky.
O wls are hooting loudly because the werewolves are coming NOW!
L aughing kids in the moonlight going trick-or-treating. They go to the
F inal house and the kids say "Happy Halloween!"

Zachary Diehl, Grade 2
Consolidated School, CT

Thanksgiving

N o one is sad on this day
O n Thanksgiving we celebrate with family and friends
V ery big turkey
E veryone loves the feast
M y family is happy
B e thankful
E veryone gives thanks on this day
R emember Thanksgiving is one day of the year

Isabella Balgobin, Grade 3
St Agatha School, NY

Shadia and Ben Forgiving Each Other

I forgive Ben because he called me names
I forgave him because he is my friend
Friends forgive each other
Ben always says he's sorry
Then I forget about what happened and Ben is nice to me
Ben makes me feel happy and glad because he forgives people
I am glad he is in my life because he is a nice friend
We are happy when we are together

Shadia Darden, Grade 3
New York Institute for Special Education, NY

Dog

Dog
dirty, disgusting
soft, warm, hard
fur, tail, skinny, big
barking, growling, whining, crying, snoring

Kyle Bottisti, Grade 2
Marie Curie Institute, NY

A Celebration of Poets – East Grades K-3 Fall 2010

Orange
Orange is one of the Gators' colors.
When I go to a Gators game, I see orange.
When the Gators win, it makes me smile.
Cole Best, Grade 2
Sweetwater Episcopal Academy, FL

Bubble Gum
Bubble gum, chomp chomp
I like the pink bubble gum
It is so juicy
Paige Farley, Grade 3
Walnut Street Elementary School, NJ

My Turtle
My turtle's pretty.
The turtle is very slow.
He goes on the rock.
Anayeli Nieto, Grade 3
Walnut Street Elementary School, NJ

Dog
It barks all the time
It chases and catches balls
I love petting them.
Nuriel David, Grade 3
Yeshiva Ketana of Long Island, NY

Ken and the Dragon
Ken met a dragon.
He turned Ken crispy and black.
The dragon was mean.
Samuel Cook, Grade 3
Walnut Street Elementary School, NJ

Fall
Leaves fall in the fall
Many colors on the trees
basically no leaves
Menachem Gewirtz, Grade 3
Yeshiva Ketana of Long Island, NY

My Friend
My friend's name is Paige
my friend is pleasant and nice
my friend is awesome
Ally Mahon, Grade 3
Walnut Street Elementary School, NJ

Soccer Fun
Soccer, fantastic
My foot is flexible when
I kick the blue ball.
Nicole Sinton, Grade 3
Walnut Street Elementary School, NJ

Snow
Snowy mountain tops
I see a pat of butter
when the sun comes up
Avrohom Yaakov Pam, Grade 3
Yeshiva Ketana of Long Island, NY

Thanksgiving
Thanksgiving is the
best, this holiday you throw
an outstanding fest
Gavin McLaughlin, Grade 3
Walnut Street Elementary School, NJ

Bubble Gum
Bubble gum is pink
it can be really messy
it is really good
Jessie Pedre, Grade 3
Walnut Street Elementary School, NJ

The Beach
It has sharks and fish
there are many waves and boats
the sand burns my feet.
Yaacov Jacobowitz, Grade 3
Yeshiva Ketana of Long Island, NY

High Merit Poems – Grades K, 1, 2, and 3

Books!
Books can be long and books can be short.
Some people may not like reading, but I insist you do,
for reading is all the subjects of school, and
if you read you're ready for the…BIG…BAD…WORLD!

The quest to finish a book is like the race against time.
Panicky…Depressing…Alone.
And with a swish of shoes and the clank of feet,
I end my poem in a happy leap.

Enyojo Agene, Grade 2
St John the Apostle Catholic School, VA

Red
Red is wonderful.
Red is the feeling of angry people.
Red is the sound of cheering for the Phillies!
Red is the sound of a cardinal tweeting.
Red is the color of a bouncing beach ball.
Red is the American flag waving in the wind,
It's the color of red hair going by.
Red is part of the rainbow way up high.
Red is blazing fire!!

Kyle Zabel, Grade 2
Interboro GATE Program, PA

Santa's Cookie Treat
Tasty, spicy, treats in the oven remind me of Christmas.
Out of the oven,
They sit on a plate waiting for Santa to eat them on Christmas Eve.
All of a sudden, they felt a shake.
The gingerbread men were gone.
Santa ate them all up!

Emma Marshall, Grade 3
Riverton Public School, NJ

Bats
B ats are soaring through the black sky.
A lmost every night you can hear their wide wings flapping.
T hey are looking for juicy fruit to eat for dinner.
S orry the night is over, but tomorrow you can wake up and eat again!
HAPPY HALLOWEEN!

Benjamin Ficarra, Grade 2
Consolidated School, CT

A Celebration of Poets – East Grades K-3 Fall 2010

My Grandmother

Every Thanksgiving when my grandmother gets out of bed
She spills gravy all over her head.
When she goes into the bathroom to wash
She puts on her best dress and then squirts on squash!
Then when she comes to meet us at two
We laugh and we laugh and she says, "puru!"
Once when we went to her house to have dinner
She ate so much, she thought she should get thinner.
Then when we went to bed that night
She asked us if we could turn on the light.
So we got up and went into a room
And watched TV the whole night through.
...I am thankful for my grandmother.

Cecelia Winn, Grade 3
Helderberg Christian School, NY

The Yellow Fellow

Yellow is the color of my hair.
Lemons are yellow. Sometimes sweet or sour.
The sun is yellow; bright, bright yellow.
There are signs on the street that are yellow.
In school I have a yellow folder.
My room is painted yellow.
I love it so much.
Pencils are yellow.
Sometimes books can be yellow.
Balloons can be yellow.
Yellow!
Yellow!
Yellow!

Jackie Pelloni, Grade 2
Sweetwater Episcopal Academy, FL

My Life as a Pilgrim

My life as a Pilgrim
There is a lot of stuff to do on land and boat.
It is fun being a Pilgrim because you can hunt.
And even make cloth for a bunch of things.
There are a lot of games to play on land.
We started the voyage in 1620 and we landed after 65 days at sea.
The feast started in 1921.

Ryan Szabo, Grade 3
St Mary School, NY

High Merit Poems – Grades K, 1, 2, and 3

October
Falling down colored leaves
Harvesting pumpkins
Raking leaves for jumping
Celebrating Columbus Day and Halloween
Dylan Morris, Grade 2
Weston Elementary School, NJ

Dogs
Balls, tug ropes, chew toys
Food dishes, leashes, beds
Playing, running, barking
Dogs
Sarah Kate Colucci, Grade 2
Weston Elementary School, NJ

Trees
Bark, leaves, roots
Red, yellow, green
Fall, winter, spring
Trees
Victoria Santana, Grade 2
Weston Elementary School, NJ

The Rainbow
The rainbow is pretty
The rainbow is all the colors in the world
The rainbow is in the sky
The rainbow comes after rain
Kaitlin Elizabeth Gervais, Grade 3
Clover Street School, CT

Dog
Cute, nice
Running, barking, sleeping
She rests in the sun a lot
Princess
Nevaeh Melendez, Grade 2
William M Meredith School, PA

My Scooter
My scooter takes me places
like my grandma's house sometimes.
It's the only place I take it
and then it takes me home.
Julissa Torres, Grade 1
Windsor Learning Academy, FL

Toys
Toy trucks
Orange balls
Yellow yo-yos
Stretchy slinkys
Destiny Medrano, Grade 2
Marie Curie Institute, NY

Daddy
Nice, handsome
Caring, helping, cooking
My Daddy loves me.
Papa
Abiona Flora, Grade 2
William M Meredith School, PA

My Leaf
My leaf is brown and spiky
With spiny wrinkly skin
It is shaped like an arrow
The edges crinkle in.
Kole Baker, Grade 2
Carlyle C Ring Elementary School, NY

Fall
Leaves are falling in the sky
Fall is fun!
My sister and I will look
At the colorful leaves
Maggie Li, Grade 2
Children's Village, PA

Bored as a Lion

I'm as bored as a lazy lion
Or a pile of dirt near a grave
I'm as angry as a troll
Or elephant in a tiny cage
Lina is as happy as a pixie
Joe is as suspicious as a spy
Heidi is as sad as a shipwreck
Jim just has one eye
Sharon thinks she knows it all
Emmy thinks she can make an elephant fall
At gym we had to do a race with three feet
I was against Ally and John they were easy to beat
Lucy wrote a poem all about blue
And Diana heard a song with only the words I do
Sianna and she could never say know
Plus Ruby's mom taught her how to sew

I'm as bored as a desk sitting still all day
or sand watching the sea
swing and sway

Iman Acharya, Grade 3
William M Meredith School, PA

The Noises of Winter

I listen…I hear …whooooooo!
I see…the whirling wind twirling zig-zag

I listen…I hear…tck-tck-tck
I see…a squirrel sucking on a nut

I listen…I hear…HE, HE, HE.
I see…joyful kids giggling

I listen…I hear…whoooooo! tck-tck-tck, HE HE HE

I see…

The whirling wind twirling,
A squirrel sucking on a nut, and
Joyful kids giggling!

Emma Rosenbaum, Grade 3
Memorial School, NH

High Merit Poems – Grades K, 1, 2, and 3

Corn/Food
Corn
Crunchy, tasty
Starting, eating, finishing
I am finished eating!
Food
Danielle Swanson, Grade 3
Kane Area Elementary/Middle School, PA

Halloween/Holiday
Halloween
Dark, spooky
Treating, scaring, walking
I am eating candy.
Holiday
Alyssa Oakes, Grade 3
Kane Area Elementary/Middle School, PA

Leaves/Fall
Leaves
Yellow, red
Falling, blowing, jumping
Walking on crunchy leaves
Fall
Hannah Gullifer, Grade 3
Kane Area Elementary/Middle School, PA

Squirrels/Chipmunk
Squirrels
Tiny, fast
Running, climbing, hiding
Squirrels like big nuts.
Chipmunk
Ainsley Saf, Grade 3
Kane Area Elementary/Middle School, PA

Fall/Autumn
Fall
Colorful, colder
Playing, working, running
The leaves are pretty.
Autumn
Victoria Hallberg, Grade 3
Kane Area Elementary/Middle School, PA

Candy/Junk food
Candy
Tasty, gummy
Eating, chewing, munching
Candy is very good.
Junk food
Raeann Asel, Grade 3
Kane Area Elementary/Middle School, PA

Skeleton/Bones
Skeleton
White, bony
Scaring, screaming, running
The kids are scared!
Bones
Mason Feikls, Grade 3
Kane Area Elementary/Middle School, PA

Monsters/Halloween
Monsters
Big, scary
Crying, running, sleeping
Monsters are very scary!
Halloween
Mackenzie Shrubb, Grade 3
Kane Area Elementary/Middle School, PA

Candy/Sugar
Candy
Tasty, sweet
Eating, chewing, munching
Candy is very good!
Sugar
Lexi Novosel, Grade 3
Kane Area Elementary/Middle School, PA

Fall Is Here!
I see pumpkins
I hear branches moving
I smell apples
I feel wind
I taste pumpkin seeds
Amelia Kramer, Grade 1
McKinley Elementary School, PA

A Celebration of Poets – East Grades K-3 Fall 2010

Dogs
Dogs are sweet
Dogs get treats
Dogs get everything
They want to eat!!
Bark! Bark! Bark!
Emma Lauryn Capuano, Grade 3
Clover Street School, CT

Me
K arate
E xcellent
L ucky
L ittle
Y o yo
Kelly Sevor, Kindergarten
Sweetwater Episcopal Academy, FL

The Sun
The sun is bright and yellow
It gives us heat and light
Sometimes the light is blocked by clouds
We all share the sun!
I like the sun!
Julia Hoffman, Grade 3
Clover Street School, CT

Texas
T errific pools
E ating delicious food
e **X** cellent houses
A wesome water parks
S uper place
Griffin Bowers, Grade 3
Shady Grove Elementary School, PA

Horse
Horse
dirty horrible
smooth furry soft
brown hair body eyes
eats walks drinks wags swats
Ashley Marrero, Grade 2
Marie Curie Institute, NY

Logan
L oves grapes
O nly seven years old
G lasses on him
A fraid of darkness
N ice
Logan Slezak, Grade 2
Marie Curie Institute, NY

Tiger
T eeth are sharp
I s a big cat
G oes fast
E ats meat
R eally scary
Jorge Ortiz, Grade 2
Marie Curie Institute, NY

A Dragon's Roar
The thump of the wings
The speed of the tail
The strength of the jaw
The heat of the fire
Watch as it rushes into the night sky.
Trent Barnecott, Grade 3
Sweetwater Episcopal Academy, FL

Josie
J umping around
O range and black are her favorite colors
S illy actor
I nside playing video games
E ats eggs or yogurt for breakfast
Josie Smith, Grade 2
Marie Curie Institute, NY

Me
K id
Y oung
L oving
E ntertainer
E qual
Kylee Szabo, Kindergarten
Sweetwater Episcopal Academy, FL

High Merit Poems – Grades K, 1, 2, and 3

My Brother
My friend is so tall
He is taller than a wall
My brother is so lame
He is still on the wall of fame

My brother was so proud
He got too loud
My brother had a can
He hit me with a pan
Elijah Jones, Grade 3
Bensley Elementary School, VA

Ice Cream
I ncredible
C reamy
E xcellent

C old
R efreshing
E xtremely good
A mazing
M elty
Brooke Berry, Grade 3
Shady Grove Elementary School, PA

My Dartmoor Pony, Cal
A horse is like a pal
I named mine Cal
She went clip, clop, clip, clop
I taught Cal a course because
She is my favorite horse!
Kathryn Hickman, Grade 3
Interboro GATE Program, PA

Thanksgiving
F all
A pple pie
M ayflower
I ndians
L et's give thanks
Y ams
Hannah Hinds, Grade 2
St Agatha School, NY

Halloween Creeps
Halloween is really creepy
And now it's time to get really freaky
We walk onto the mat
Then we see a black cat
We go trick-or-treating
Then we start eating
We see a mouse
In a creepy house
The witch is flying near the moon
I hope I see her soon!
A ghost flew among the stars
Is he quite far?
Halloween, Halloween
What a wonderful scene!
Turiya Moka, Grade 2
Wellington School, FL

Snow
First is morning
Then comes the snow.
It's time to go play.
Snow is falling.
Snow is falling.
The snow is white and fluffy.
It's almost like Christmas
Except it's not.
It is s-o-o-o-o cold outside.
I should put on a scarf,
Two mittens,
A winter jacket,
And some boots.
Now I am ready to go outside.
Ashley Gray, Grade 3
Eagle's View Academy, FL

Trees/Leaves
Trees
Orange, yellow
Falling, raking, jumping
The pile was gone!
Leaves
Zackary Howe, Grade 3
Kane Area Elementary/Middle School, PA

My Special Rock

So tiny, so light
So colorful, so bright

My rock, my special rock,
I will always keep.
Special — because
It's shaped like a K.

The rock I've always wanted
Brings me good luck.
That's worth way more than a buck

I love my rock — my special rock.
Katherine Violette, Grade 3
Memorial School, NH

My Pal

I have a little something
Big ears has he
But not a lemur or a bat
His color is champagne
But he's not a drink
His eyes are blue
But not a baby is he!
His ears are tall
But he's not a bunny
His nose is cold
AND
He's a Chihuahua
And my best pal!
Cora Sheppard, Grade 3
Mary Walter Elementary School, VA

Thanksgiving

I like Thanksgiving
N ovember is awesome
D ads and moms gather the food
I give thanks
A pple pie
N obody misses the feast
S hare the turkey
Antonio Schoenhardt, Grade 2
St Agatha School, NY

My Ballerina Pumpkin

My beautiful purple ballerina.
Her name is Christina.
She has a pretty pink dress.
She can dance all the rest.
She is so sweet.
She can dance to the beat.
Christie Alvarez, Grade 3
Coral Springs Elementary School, FL

When Is Thanksgiving?

When fat turkeys gobble.
When sweet apple pie gets sliced.
When Autumn leaves fall.
When yummy good gets cooked.
Then it's Thanksgiving!
Grazie!
Alexander Iacono, Grade 3
Triangle Elementary School, NJ

I'm Thankful

Blue sky means bright and sunny
Red sky means sunrise or sunset
Black sky means twilight or night
Gray sky means rainy or gloomy
A smile on my face means
I'm thankful for all color skies.
Jacob R. Finello, Grade 3
St Mary's School, NJ

Snow

S ome people like to play outside
N ever go out without your coat
O n the news it will tell you it's 20 degrees
W ith your ice skates you go skating
Selena Rivera, Grade 3
Northeast Elementary School, NY

I Like Green

I like green toys
I like green k'nex
I like green Legos
Junhao Zhao, Grade 1
Children's Village, PA

High Merit Poems – Grades K, 1, 2, and 3

The Race
As I go up to the gate
I'm wide awake
I got there first
Everyone else must be cursed
I hit a bump
I get to the jump
As I went around the track
My back begins to crack
I'm finished with the laps
The crowd claps
I go to my trailer from the race
I have sweat pouring down my face
As I got home
I see that my trophy was made of chrome
Scott Daley, Grade 3
Mary Walter Elementary School, VA

My Life as a Wampanoag Boy
As a Wampanoag boy
I live in Massachusetts near the bay
I sleep in a wetu at night
And like to fish all day

I love my parents
And they love me
They teach me how to hunt
And fish in the sea

My new friends come from Europe
They are called Pilgrims
I play new games with my new friends
My favorite game is nine pins
Liam McGoldrick, Grade 3
St Mary School, NY

Fall Is Here!
I see pumpkins
I hear wind blowing
I smell apple pie
I feel cold air
I taste pumpkin pie
Brian Thai, Grade 1
McKinley Elementary School, PA

Haylan's Halloween
It was All Hallows Eve
We had gone out to trick-or-treat
Leaving Mom home with Haylan
To make witch's stew with meat

A call came in to Dad
Mom had quite a fright
Haylan smashed his big toe
It was a very long night

Haylan went to sleep
To the hospital the next day
The doctors worked hard
He'd be just fine they would say

Baby Haylan came home
We were relieved you can bet
It was one Halloween night
We won't soon forget!
Ansley Haught, Grade 3
St Alexis School, PA

Things That Make Me Go Wow
Let me tell you how
What makes me go wow
Colorado mountains
New York City fountains
Roller coaster rides
And the changing tides
Getting a new pet
Catching a fish in a net
When my mom goes shopping
I get a new jump rope for hopping
I love to have pillow fights
With my sisters in the night
When I score a soccer goal
I fell like I found some gold
Jumping on my mothers bed
When she finds us we play dead
These are just a few things
That makes my heart sing
Victoria Mangelli, Grade 3
Bayville Intermediate School, NY

Barbie Dolls
My Barbie dolls
Are so cute
I play with them
Night and day
They make me happy
While I play
I have so much fun
I wish I would never be done
Mia Scandrett, Kindergarten
Windsor Learning Academy, FL

Spiky Leaf
Dark yellow with black spots
Little holes, it has lots
In the middle a big dent
My old leaf is bent
Spiky points on all the sides
In the wind it smoothly glides
My leaf will soon be dust
By human foot be crushed.
Kyler Houghwot, Grade 2
Carlyle C Ring Elementary School, NY

Beach
Sand
Boats
Seashells
Boardwalk
Swimming
Big waves
Rocks
Ocean
Connor Hagan, Grade 2
Weston Elementary School, NJ

Gymnastics
Bounce, bounce, bounce
On the trampoline
Round, round, round
On the bars
Flip, flip, flip
On the floor
Dip, dip, dip
On the beam
Makenzie Besse, Grade 2
Carlyle C Ring Elementary School, NY

Cheerleading
Pom-poms
Uniform
Dancing
Megaphones
Inside or outside
Competition
Leading cheers
Cheerleading
Holly Cornelson, Grade 2
Weston Elementary School, NJ

I Like Red
I like red.
A book is red.
A toy is red.
A crayola is red.
Sometimes the words are red.
Sometimes the leaves are red.
I love red.
Ivan Zeng, Grade 2
Children's Village, PA

Goldfish
Gold fish
watery, slippery
shining, swimming, sliding
swimming around the tank
Pet fish
Joshua DelValle, Grade 3
Marie Curie Institute, NY

Ball
Ball
rubber, hard
flinging, whipping, passing
you can play with it
Pigskin.
Donavin McClanahan, Grade 3
Marie Curie Institute, NY

High Merit Poems – Grades K, 1, 2, and 3

Mom

Mom I love you so so much
I want you to stay for lunch
And we can munch our lunch together
I love you so…much!!!

Trinity Arzu, Grade 1
Public School 121x The Throop School, NY

Fall

Falling leaves
And apple pies
Little animals scurrying
Late into the night

Samuel Robinson, Grade 2
Worthington Hooker School – K-2 Campus, CT

Cheetahs

Cheetahs
Fast and fearless
Vicious and deadly
Cheetahs

Aristotle Powell, Grade 2
Worthington Hooker School – K-2 Campus, CT

Swimming

When I feel the water it makes me feel calm.
When I swim I feel the cool breeze.
It is the best feeling in the world!
It makes me feel relaxed.

Tiara Skinner, Grade 2
Carlyle C Ring Elementary School, NY

Cell

C ells are in living things
E very cell has a cell membrane
L ots of cells are in people
L ittle

Carter Bixby, Grade 3
Susquehanna Community Elementary School, PA

My Mom and Me

I love my mom
She's good to me
Hugs me and kisses me.

She plays with me on the computer.
We play Nick, Jr.
She cooks my favorite food too.
Hot dogs!

She's so pretty when she gets dressed up and
I share my toys and puzzles with her.
She makes silly faces and does silly dances.

I feel happy she's here.
I feel good because I love her.

It's a good thing she's in my life.
She respects me.
She cares about me
That's my mom and me.

Keisha Vilela-Ortiz, Grade 1
New York Institute for Special Education, NY

The First Thanksgiving

ONLY the rocks remember
The first day of Thanksgiving
The Pilgrims were busy on the MAYFLOWER
A storm whipped the ocean for more than an hour
Now that storm has lots of power
The Mayflower swirled out to sea
That storm is really ugly
Soon the ship gets to shore
The Pilgrims soon own this land
They met Squanto and his brother
They say they lost their mother
Squanto holds up two arrows
One means peace and one means war
The Pilgrims chose peace
The Indians say it's time to eat
So they kill animals and have a feast.

Matthew Esposito, Grade 3
Jeffrey Elementary School, CT

High Merit Poems – Grades K, 1, 2, and 3

Lettuce
I make you strong
So you live long
But do you wash me clean?
I'm green
I am good with ham in a sandwich
Can you guess what I am?
Yes, lettuce
David Romero, Grade 2
Mary Walter Elementary School, VA

Bubblegum
bubble bubbly bubblegum
chew it hard
chew it soft
make it flat
stick your tongue through it
blow, bubble!
blow the bubble, bubble!
Emily Capofreddi, Grade 3
Thoreau Elementary School, MA

Parks
Swings, slides, tires
Mulch, grass, sand
Laughter, fun, excitement
Babies, toddlers, children
Butterflies, birds, worms
Trees, flowers, bushes
Parks
Alexis Abbott, Grade 2
Weston Elementary School, NJ

Playing with George
I love to play with George.
He really is my friend.
Frisbee is a game we play.

We play all kinds of games.
When we are on the swings
we fly to outer space.
Ashton Gagne, Grade 1
Windsor Learning Academy, FL

A Halloween Fright
One Halloween night,
I had a fright.
I was asking for treats,
When my heart skipped a few beats.

A ghost tapped on my back,
And asked for a snack.
My eyes got real wide,
And I ran inside.

He followed me in,
And down went my chin.
I gave him a sucker,
That made his mouth pucker.

The ghost was so happy,
Then he got nappy.
So I said goodbye,
And tried not to cry.
Sarah Randig, Grade 3
St Alexis School, PA

Begin with Porcelain
Her name is Polly
And she's my dolly.

She came from Holland
For my fifth birthday.

Of porcelain she's made;
Her color will not fade.

But she can be broken,
So on the shelf she lies.

She has a pink dress and a hat
White shoes and that

Is why I'm knitting her a sweater.
Can you think of something better?
Madeleine DeWitt, Kindergarten
The American Academy, PA

A Walk in Fall

I was walking along
And I was singing a song.
I came to a tree,
It was very big compared to me.

Red, yellow and orange but no green,
It was the prettiest tree I have ever seen!
I looked up at it and spotted a squirrel,
I didn't know if it was a boy or a girl.

The squirrel dropped an acorn on my head,
It was small but it felt like lead!
I kept walking, enjoying the weather
When down from the sky drifted a feather.

The feather was brown and it came from a hawk.
I was almost done with my walk.
My walk is over; I'm at my door
I wish I had time to walk some more.

Joseph Wiethorn, Grade 3
St Alexis School, PA

The Night I Got Lost

Lips of black boom
My sentence of death
In the woods
The sound of the violin fills my soul
Blood runs like a waterfall rushing down against me
In a cave black bats tremble and dart around my head
Again and again
A dragon sleeps in a hole of dull and gray and snores
Again and again

Then I stare in horror at a ghostly silvery shape
As it moves closer and closer
I freeze
The ghost just floated there for a minute
"What are you doing here?"
I murmur, "I got lost and can't get home."
The ghost says, "Poor thing, I will help you."
And she brings me all the way home.

Riley Tattersall, Grade 3
Oak Ridge Elementary School, PA

High Merit Poems – Grades K, 1, 2, and 3

Kaleidoscope of the Maple Tree

Maple tree, maple tree
You are my most favorite tree.
You are a popular tree.

Maple tree one of America's
Most popular trees.
You are in cities, communities and towns.
You provide shade and syrup to all.

You have an aroma that makes anyone shiver,
You change your color and give us flavor.

In winter you are white
In spring you are yellow
In fall you are green
In summer you are red.

Maple tree, maple tree
You are the prettiest tree of all.

Janine Hammond, Grade 2
Public School 235 Janice Marie Knight, NY

My Little Tree

Tree, Tree, Tree
You small deciduous tree.
You'll always mean so much to me

Tree, Tree, Tree
Oh dear, you sweetie
Even though you are sterile
And do not produce fruit,
The birds still love you very much.

Tree, Tree, Tree
You mean so much to me
Because in fall your leaves change
To a bright and purple red.
That brightens up my little shed.

Parris Jade Comrie, Grade 2
Public School 235 Janice Marie Knight, NY

Friends

I like you
You like me
We all like each other as you can see
We share, we care, we love one another
We share our love all together
So jump right on in so you can be loved too,
No matter what the weather.

Jeremiah Acosta, Grade 3
Number 12 Elementary School, NJ

Fall

Leaves changing colors; yellow, red, green and brown
And falling to the ground,
Pumpkins, apples, and apple cider cooking in my mom's house,
The squirrels crunching on their acorns,
And the beautiful leaves falling from the trees,
Nuts, acorns, and squirrels getting on my hand,
A nice juicy apple in my mouth!

Brianna Cavalieri, Grade 2
Wellington School, FL

Butch

Butch is my dog
He is a Shih Tzu
He's black and white too
I love to play with him
And he barks a lot when he gets a trim
Sometimes he chews on my shoe
I wonder what he thinks when I scare him and say boo

Gianna Mendiola, Grade 3
St James School, NJ

Subway

When I'm in the mood for a bologna sandwich,
I'll be going to subway,
To hear the chefs crumble the bread,
To watch the chefs make my sandwich,
While I wait to eat my sandwich,
I'll be back again next weekend,
When I'm in the mood for a bologna sandwich.

Austin Armer, Grade 3
Marie Curie Institute, NY

High Merit Poems – Grades K, 1, 2, and 3

The Sea of Sleep
The sea of sleep
Will sleep tonight,
The sea of sleep
Under moonlight.
The ocean sways
Under the sky,
I wish I could
Call it mine.
Whisper songs of wisdom
Sing softly in the wind,
I wonder if anything
Will be more beautiful than this.
Tatum Courtmanche, Grade 3
Jeffrey Elementary School, CT

Autumn Night
Autumn night and all is silent
Not one sound from the air to the ground
Only the wind whispering
And whistling in my ear
All night long as the moon shimmered
On the sparkling bright light lake
As bright as the sun
You can see frogs jump high
As the roof and graceful as a party gown
And as everyone says goodnight
The moon falls into a deep sleep
Under the blanket of shiny stars.
Sophia Fedus, Grade 3
Jeffrey Elementary School, CT

My Sister
She likes to act cool
But hates school
She likes to bite
And to fly a kite

She likes to ride her bike
And she likes to hike
She was born in the year of the monkey
And she is really funky
Tiffani Roberts, Grade 3
Bensley Elementary School, VA

Snow Time
It is time for snow to come,
down from the sky.
It is nice to have snow.
You can make something out of it.
A snow angel, a snow man,
and a snow ball fight.
Snow is fun.
We are glad that we have snow.
Thank you God for the world.
Alexa White, Grade 3
Our Lady of Hope School, NY

Can You?
Can you slither like a snake?
Can you hop like a bunny?
Can you bite like a shark?
Can you hop like a frog?
Can you chomp like a crocodile?
Can you fly like a bird?
Can you stay as still as a clam?
As still as that?
Can you?
Angela Brave, Grade 1
Blessed Sacrament School, FL

Dogs
Dogs
Fuzzy, nice
Running, chasing, jumping
Dogs can be smelly
Pet
Alanis Seeley, Grade 3
Marie Curie Institute, NY

Thanksgiving
F ood
A pple pie
M y Thanksgiving
I ndians
L ots of turkey
Y ou give thanks
Alexandra Conaboy, Grade 1
St Agatha School, NY

Happy Halloween
Witches in the dark.
Scary ghosts popping out now.
Halloween is cool!
Eric Giraldo, Grade 2
Wanamassa Elementary School, NJ

Halloween Is Coming
Here come spooky times.
I like to jump in leaves.
Halloween is cool.
Matthew Shaw, Grade 2
Wanamassa Elementary School, NJ

October Fun!
My birthday is here!
Goblins are spooky at night.
The candy tastes good.
Mollie Nirschl, Grade 2
Wanamassa Elementary School, NJ

Fall
I like Halloween!
Leaves are cool and beautiful.
Pumpkins everywhere!
Kevin Novobilsky, Grade 2
Wanamassa Elementary School, NJ

Here Comes Halloween!
I love Halloween.
Monsters are under your bed.
Bats are in the sky.
Carisa Graziano, Grade 2
Wanamassa Elementary School, NJ

Halloween Fun
Halloween is fun.
Spooky witches are coming.
I like to dress up.
Brooke Barker, Grade 2
Wanamassa Elementary School, NJ

My Blues
Blue is the crayon I use at school
Blue is the water in the pool
Blue is the sky
Above the dessert so dry
Blue is the blue berry so sweet
Blue is the color of my soccer cleat
Blue is the color of daffodil
Blue is the color of my sand pail
This is my blues
What is yours?
Abel Varghese, Grade 3
Beltsville Academy, MD

The Wave Pool
I love to be pushed
by the waves.
It is fun to swim around.
I swim down to the bottom
but have to come back up for air.

When the waves aren't pushing me
I get to relax.
At the end of the day
I'm tired and then I can go home.
Aryella Marti, Grade 1
Windsor Learning Academy, FL

Reindeer
I see reindeers eating, flying, jumping,
playing and searching for food.
I hear those bells ringing.
I see one reindeer sleeping and snoring.
Santa comes to his sleigh he sees
the reindeer eating, flying, jumping,
playing and searching for food.
Then he puts the reindeer hooked up
to his sleigh and then they're all
flying in the sky.
Juliana Izzo, Grade 3
Our Lady of Hope School, NY

High Merit Poems – Grades K, 1, 2, and 3

Ocean, Stream, River, Waterfall
Water bounces across its rocks
To join its same identical twins
It flows across green, brown, black, blue and white
More come to meet it
More is fearless
It passes all
Travels across the world even as it freezes
But soon it will continue its course
Everlasting journey fast or slow
It still travels

Dylan Cassidy, Grade 3
Jeffrey Elementary School, CT

Friends
My friends will never let me down.
They will cheer me up when I have a frown.
We will never leave each other alone.
We like to eat ice cream cones.
We all like to play hide and seek,
even though sometimes we peek.
We all paint each others nails.
We will always be best pals,
At the end of the day we all go home,
So we talk to each other on the phone.

Emilee Synor, Grade 3
Ellicott Road Elementary School, NY

My Great Uncle Francie
My Great Uncle Francie loved me
My mom, dad, brothers, and sister
And everybody in his family
even his friends

He served in the Army but never really talked about it
He lived in Avis, Pennsylvania
He had two kids, John and Kathy
He was one of the best men I knew
I miss my Great Uncle Francie

Nick Kurtz, Grade 3
Robeson Elementary School, PA

Thankful
T urkey
H ealth
A unt
N ouns
K iss
F east and friends
U s
L ord
Connor Bankuti, Grade 1
St. Mary's School, NJ

Thankful
T hanksgiving
H arvest
A dventures
N ovember
K ittens
F aith and feast
U nited States
L aughter, Lord and love
Gabrielle Mosca, Grade 1
St Mary's School, NJ

Thankful
T urkey
H arvest
A nimals
N ovember
K ittens
F amily and friends
U nited States
L ord
Paulina Rust, Grade 1
St Mary's School, NJ

Play
Play
fun, good
running, jumping, shipping
it is fun playing
games
Anthony Darpino, Grade 3
Marie Curie Institute, NY

Football
F ootball is a hard sport
O ffense
O n the field
T ouchdown
B all
A ll of us tackle
L ine up
L eaving the stadium
Lason Troutman, Grade 3
Bensley Elementary School, VA

The United States
I like the United States
It is beautiful
California has redwood trees
New Jersey has yellow bees
In Virginia it rained a bunch
And I like to eat yummy lunch
In Pennsylvania I saw many fish
And they all went swish, swish, swish
Rishi Purohit, Kindergarten
St James School, NJ

School Spirit
I like to write big stories
that's what school spirit is to me.
It helps me be creative
and write about me.
I would rather stay inside
than go out with my friends.
It gives me more time to write
about my school spirit.
Destiny Spady, Grade 2
Windsor Learning Academy, FL

Dogs
Dogs
fun, sleep,
playing, resting, drinking
I want a dog
puppy
Sapphire Taylor, Grade 3
Marie Curie Institute, NY

Fall

Leaves changing into colors; yellow, green, and brown,
Apples hanging from the trees and pie being baked,
Leaves crunching beneath my feet,
Strawberries that are cool, icy treats,
Bark and colorful leaves on a tree,
And coats on my friends!

Mackenzie Dias, Grade 2
Wellington Academy, FL

Autumn

A utumn is when deciduous trees loose their leaves
U p on the trees leaves fall in Autumn
T he tress get ready to hibernate at the end of Autumn
U p in the sky rain falls a lot
M ost trees are deciduous
N utrients are what the trees take in

Samantha Voege, Grade 3
Susquehanna Community Elementary School, PA

Pine Cones

Pine cones
Brown layered treasures
Falling from the trees
Down rolling hills
Following the breeze
Pine cones

Aelah Meyer, Grade 2
Worthington Hooker School – K-2 Campus, CT

Snow Is Falling

It is exciting when snow is falling,
You can always make a snowman.
When you get cold, in the house you start going.
Then you could watch the snow plop on the window panes.

Jarrett Slaton, Grade 2
Virginia A Boone Highland Oaks Elementary School, FL

Life of Nature

Breeze of swaying trees
Captures life of some nature
Flowing happiness

Rachel Lieberman, Grade 2
Virginia A Boone Highland Oaks Elementary School, FL

A Celebration of Poets – East Grades K-3 Fall 2010

Cats
I see cats playing
playing, eating, having fun
I see cats chasing mice
they are very furry
so they must be shedding a lot.
Maya Kulikowski, Grade 3
Our Lady of Hope School, NY

Science
Science
sweaty fiery
wet gooey smoky
watery fiery smoky blue
explodes burns smokes crackles bubbles
Elisha Milette, Grade 2
Marie Curie Institute, NY

Tiger
Tiger
outdoors grass
soft fluffy warm
hair black orange white
walks runs jogs eats sits
Kayla Rivera, Grade 2
Marie Curie Institute, NY

Foods
F resh fish
O range oranges
O dd okra
D ozens of donuts
S unflower seeds
Margaret Martin, Grade 2
Marie Curie Institute, NY

Bears
B ears are brave not afraid
E at lots of meat
A ttack if they see you
R oar, roar
S o frightening when you see them
Laurel Vrooman, Grade 2
Marie Curie Institute, NY

School
When I'm ready to learn,
I'll be listening in school,
To hear the teacher and students,
To watch the teacher teach math,
While I write on the paper,
I'll be back again on Monday,
When I'm ready to learn.
Felix Guzman, Grade 3
Marie Curie Institute, NY

Cold
S o cold outside.
N ice shovel.
O n cold days I drink hot chocolate.
W ind blows through my hair.
M ake big snowballs.
A nice thing to do.
N ow let's have a snowball fight.
Ayana Smith, Grade 3
Northeast Elementary School, NY

Friends
F riends
R espect
I n people's houses
E nding of a story
N ew friends
D elicious food
S ummer fun
Taylor Brown, Grade 3
McKinley Elementary School, PA

Michael
M agnificent
I ndependent
C hallenging
H igh in grade
A crobatics
E xtremely Fast
L oving
Michael Castor, Grade 3
McKinley Elementary School, PA

High Merit Poems – Grades K, 1, 2, and 3

I Love Art

My favorite thing to do is art
It's lots of fun to do
I can do clay, markers and pastel crayons too
I do it every day
So could you
When I'm done I hang it up
And then I show it off

Alex Gelman, Grade 3
Shady Grove Elementary School, PA

Olive Garden

When I'm in the mood to eat salad and breadsticks,
I'll be eating at Olive Garden,
To hear the people talk and laugh,
To watch my family eat their dinner and dessert,
While I'm eating and drinking,
I'll be back again next Saturday,
When I'm in the mood for salad and breadsticks.

Jiarmani Santiago, Grade 3
Marie Curie Institute, NY

I Pulled My Sister's Hair

I pulled my sister's hair right out of her head
I pulled my sister's hair right before she went to bed
I pulled my sister's hair, because she said to me:
"You want to be a slug, that's what you want to be."
I know it sounds weird, and I was a little mean,

My sister and I made a really big scene!

Hope Karnes, Grade 2
Brookside Elementary School, NY

Monster

M ummies dancing all around.
O wls creeping on the ground.
N o one knows they are there and haunting you.
S neaky, scary monsters all over the place.
T errifying creatures in the night.
E erie noises all around.
R ude trolls making bad scary spells.

Autumn Perlman, Grade 2
Consolidated School, CT

Turkeys

T urkeys like to fly
U nder bushes they hide
R ed feathers on boys
K ids can find turkeys in the woods
E very turkey likes to run
Y ellow golden feathers on boys
S ome turkeys can jump

Jonathan Wolff, Grade 2
Marie Curie Institute, NY

Winter

Winter is my favorite season of all.
The snow falls down all gentle and soft.
The fireplace warms my hands.
All toasty and warm.
There's one now.
It falls on my tongue.
Lick, lick, lick.

Owen Maksimovich, Grade 2
Sweetwater Episcopal Academy, FL

Halloween Is Calling

Halloween is calling from here and there.
Something is yelling for me in the air
Spiders stay insiders scared of the night
The brave ones stay out late,
Then come crawling through the gate
Halloween is calling for me!!!
What scary thing is next?

Olivia Pinciaro, Grade 2
Carlyle C Ring Elementary School, NY

Football

I throw my football
To my friend
He should catch it
Or be hit
I'm sure he will be mad
At me
Because that's how it should be

Chantze Martinez, Kindergarten
Windsor Learning Academy, FL

Fall

Fall and autumn leaves are swirling.
Orange leaves are falling and the
Leaves are colorful.
The wind blows the leaves.
The leaves fall down from the trees.
Leaves are falling.
I like fall.

Michael Mei, Grade 1
Children's Village, PA

Camp

A chipmunk running across the grass
People talking
The sun was very bright
Cars going by
How long has it been there?
What made the lake?
It felt special to me

Sam Hayer, Grade 3
Warren Elementary School, VT

Fall

Fall gets cool.
All the colorful leaves
Red, green, and brown,
All fall down.
The breeze
Blows the leaves
Down.

Tyler Lee, Grade 2
Eagle's View Academy, FL

Anywhere

I like to play with my dog.
My dog is brown.
He runs around the town.
My dog is brown.
He jumps on my chair.
He runs away and I can't
find him anywhere!

Sebastian Taborda, Grade 1
Mother Seton Inter Parochial School, NJ

High Merit Poems – Grades K, 1, 2, and 3

Red

Red is fire.
Fire is hot.
Red is a fire truck.
A fire truck carries water.
Red is spicy.
Spicy is food.
Red is the color of an apple.
Apples are nice and sweet.
Red is the American Flag.
The American Flag is a true glory.
Nicky Nelson, Grade 2
Sweetwater Episcopal Academy, FL

Florida

Florida is very hot,
but I like it a lot.
I love going to the beaches,
and eating fresh peaches.
Hotels are nice places to stay,
because I like it that way.
It is nice to visit old friends,
one of my friends names is Ben.
Outside is a great place to play,
because I do it all day!
Rachael Major, Grade 3
Ellicott Road Elementary School, NY

School

I have to go to school,
that is a rule.
There is always a fuss,
on the school bus.
My bus driver gets mad,
if the children are bad.
The lunch lady makes mushroom stew,
that looks like goo!
When I go home every day,
I go outside to play.
Sean Magner, Grade 3
Ellicott Road Elementary School, NY

Mac and Cheese

I love Mac and cheese
It is awesome and tasty
It tastes cheesy good!
Nikki Millemann, Grade 3
Walnut Street Elementary School, NJ

Vampire Bat

It hangs upside down
it likes to sleep all day long
it flies in the dark.
Avi Schuckman, Grade 3
Yeshiva Ketana of Long Island, NY

Pumpkins

Pumpkin is a treat
Pumpkin pie is too yummy
I hope I eat pie
Amber Leigh Nodes, Grade 3
Walnut Street Elementary School, NJ

Snowflakes

They are light as a feather
They are so icy,
Small frozen sparkles falling.
Jordyn Lucas, Grade 3
Shady Grove Elementary School, PA

Summer

Summer is so hot
like I am near an oven
wish it was winter.
Nachi Sklar, Grade 3
Yeshiva Ketana of Long Island, NY

School

School is terrific.
My teacher's entertaining.
My class is helpful.
Jane DeNardo, Grade 3
Walnut Street Elementary School, NJ

Christmas

Christmas is cold like the Grandpa's ice cubes.
Kids get presents under the big trees.
I like the toys Santa gives me.
It is like getting charms in big boxes.

Kevin Dougherty, Grade 2
St John the Apostle Catholic School, VA

Snow

I see snow all around.
I roll the snow in a ball and make a snowman.
I put a carrot on his nose and I put cherries on his lips.
With my extra balls I will have a snow ball fight.

Amanda Zinser, Grade 3
Our Lady of Hope School, NY

Cell

C ell membrane
E nergy from food
L eaf cells make food for the plant
L iving cells have parts

Samantha Adams, Grade 3
Susquehanna Community Elementary School, PA

Cats

C ats are cute and cuddly.
A n awesome and adorable creation God made.
T hey love to play and chase mice.
S ometimes they get themselves into mischief.

Hannah Myers, Grade 1
St John Neumann Academy, VA

Statue of Liberty

I want to see the Statue of Liberty in New York city.
She welcomes people to our country.
She lights up her torch for everybody to see.
I will see her on Thanksgiving.

Samantha Flaute, Grade 2
Sweetwater Episcopal Academy, FL

Peace

Peace is relaxing
Watching a flower bloom.
Birds tweeting when I wake up.
Playing y8.
Going to the beach.
Watching Cartoon Network.
Eating ice cream.
Sleeping on my cozy couch.
But most of all,
Peace is watching a flower bloom.
Steven Ngo, Grade 3
St Augustine Cathedral School, CT

How I Promote Peace

I bring peace
by being quiet.
If someone is trying
to rest,
being quiet
is the best thing
you can do.
Being noisy
would be
being mean.
Brandon Miller, Grade 1
Our Lady of Mercy Regional School, NY

My Autumn Hike

The sun was low in the sky.
The mountain looked rocky and bumpy.

I started climbing, stretching.
I was with Longwalk and Chowhound.
They called me Snackpack.

He crashed on the mountain in the war.
I built a stack of rocks in his honor.
His name was Audie Murphy.
Jacob Lake, Grade 1
St John Neumann Academy, VA

Bees

I love the bees!
In the leaves,
Bees are free
Like we.

With their honey,
They are so sunny.
In the air
They are so fair.

A bear
Is not fair!
He steals
A great deal.

When the pollen
Is fallen,
All the bees
Go for tea.
Emma Gómez, Grade 1
Home School, FL

My Sister*

I love when my sister
Screams and smiles
at the same time
I love the way she
looks at me
My sister loves me
like I love her
She sticks her
Tongue out at me
And opens her eyes wide
It's almost like
she wants me to
pick her up!
My sister!
Jordan Henry Pabon, Grade 3
Clover Street School, CT
*Inspired by the Poets' Corner Poets

Things I Like
Summer
Christmas
Halloween
Horses
Birthdays
Toys
Candy
Purple
Parties
Water parks
These are things I like
Yekaterina Saburova, Grade 2
Weston Elementary School, NJ

Soccer Ball
S occer is my favorite sport
O h, my trophy is so sweet
C all the players to the field
C oach, could I start in the game
E ach player has practiced
R oll the ball

B oys are good at soccer
A ll kids should play soccer
L et's win the game
L aughing after the game
Brian Luna, Grade 3
Bensley Elementary School, VA

Fish
I like to fish.
You can catch fish.
Fish are cool.
Fish are slimy.
Fish are big.
Fish are heavy.
I just can't stop because I love fish.
It is hard to catch fish.
We sometimes catch fish with nets.
I love fish.
It is fun to catch them.
Brenden Parker, Grade 2
Sweetwater Episcopal Academy, FL

I Am Purple
I am purple.
I come from a vine.
My vine is green.
I am sweet.
I am sour.
I am delicious.
I have seeds inside me.
I don't come from a tree.
I am healthy.
I am beautiful.
What am I...?
Kelsey Hurtado, Grade 1
Northeast Elementary School, NY

Ladybugs
Ladybugs, ladybugs,
I love ladybugs.
Red, orange and yellow.

I gave them some jello and grass
And raisins soaked in sugar.
Really, really cute and tiny.

A lot of ladybugs everywhere,
In my house — I don't care,
In my hair — they are everywhere.
Sarah Murphy, Grade 1
St. James School, NJ

Fall
Fall is a ball.
There is so much to do,
Like raking leaves
Red, yellow, and green too.
We jump in the leaves.
We rake them again.
And we do this again and again.
We have lots of fun.
We wear jackets too.
We love to feel the breeze
And a little sun, too.
Taylor Schnorbus, Grade 2
Eagle's View Academy, FL

High Merit Poems – Grades K, 1, 2, and 3

Fruit in Summer: Jam in Winter

In the summer my mother, my sister, and I
Went searching for fruit in the orchards nearby.

Plums, apricots, peaches, and blackberries, too,
One fruit a week, our stash grew and grew.

First we picked strawberries from plants on the ground,
The berries were bright, juicy and round.

Next we picked blackberries from a tall bush,
If I held them tight, I felt them go squish.

Riding home in the car, the fruit on my lap,
I ate a few plums and took a good nap.

Before making jam, I washed fruit for my mother.
"Peaches, please! Can't I just have another?"

"No more now! The fruit is all measured.
We'll put jam in jars, and it will be treasured."

"Can I stir?" Mom said, "You may NOT!"
"This jam has to boil. It gets very hot!"

I sat on a stool and watched the jam boil.
I thought of the fruit that grew from the soil.

The season for summer fruit goes so fast,
But jars of jam make summer's taste last.

Laura Null, Grade 3
The American Academy, PA

Football

F ootball is fun
O h so fun to play with friends
O oo how they cheer
T ouchdown is near
B alance is key
A h don't drop that ball
L inebackers hold that defensive line
L ook, now, touchdown

Christopher Conyers, Grade 1
Gilmore Memorial Christian Academy, NJ

A Celebration of Poets – East Grades K-3 Fall 2010

Matthew Voutsinos
Matthew
Caring and fun
Sibling of Ava
Lover of ice cream and chocolate
Who fears spiders and snakes
Who would like to see outer space and Greece
Resident of Elkins Park, PA
Voutsinos

Matthew Voutsinos, Grade 3
McKinley Elementary School, PA

Ava
Ava
Sporty and sassy
Sibling of younger brother Drew
Lover of the Phillies and the beach
Who fears bees and the dark
Who like to see San Diego and Hollywood, CA
Resident of Elkins Park, PA
Paxson

Ava Paxson, Grade 3
McKinley Elementary School, PA

Julie
Julie
Caring and funny
Sibling of Aaron
Lover of Bradley the cat and roller coasters
Who fears bugs and mascots
Who would like to see the Statue of Liberty and Niagara Falls
Resident of Elkins Park, PA
Perlman

Julie Perlman, Grade 3
McKinley Elementary School, PA

Winter Holidays
Can you see the snow falling?
Can you hear the jingle bells?
Can you smell the gingerbread?
Can you taste the hot cocoa?
Can you feel the toasty fire?

Adora Saro, Grade 2
Worthington Hooker School – K-2 Campus, CT

Cell

C ells are cool
E ntire world has cells
L ots of cells on the world
L ots of cells make up us

Shane Muiter, Grade 3
Susquehanna Community Elementary School, PA

Winter

I'm going to tell you about winter.
Here are two things I'm going to explain.
Winter is cold, so cold,
So cold, you might complain!

Gabriel Greenspan, Grade 2
Virginia A Boone Highland Oaks Elementary School, FL

Special Things

Mom — Mom, I love Christina, Sonia, Terrell, Kelly, and Juli.
My flowers like water and sleep and sunshine and singing.
Mom — Mom buys bread and water and rice cakes, and candy for my family.
Because it is a special treat for us and I love them all.

Christina McCain, Grade 1
J.C. Stuart Elementary School, NJ

Fall

F luttering leaves in the
A utumn season.
L eaf piles are fun to jump in.
L it up jack-o-lanterns light up the dark sky.

Tyler Halas, Grade 2
Consolidated School, CT

Spinach

When you eat spinach you can never go wrong
Spinach makes you healthy and strong
This is Popeye's food when he's in a bad mood
Spinach is good, dude

Colton Friesen, Grade 2
Mary Walter Elementary School, VA

Me
Nicole
Nice and creative
Owner of Buddy, the dog
Lover of peanuts and dogs
Who hopes to excel in third grade
Who would like to travel to Hawaii
Resident of Pennsylvania
Melchiorre
Nicole Melchiorre, Grade 3
McKinley Elementary School, PA

Super Pumpkin
Super pumpkin round and orange
He fights crime in the mornings,
And in the nights too!
He is so busy!
He never sleeps.
When he is really, really sleepy,
He hides inside an old dog house.
Where he can fall asleep!
Ethan Bissoondial, Grade 3
Coral Springs Elementary School, FL

I Have a Lot to Be Thankful For
There is a turkey on the table,
so much food there is a lot.
I am glad that I am able
to give thanks for all I got.
All the family all together,
standing up or sitting down.
They would come whatever weather,
now they're here, they're all around.
Olivia Phillips, Grade 3
Birches Elementary School, NJ

Softball
S afe
O ut
F un
T imeout
B ase
A thletic
L ove it!
L eft field
Jailyn Murphy, Grade 3
Wapping Elementary School, CT

Can You?
Can you chomp like a crocodile?
Can you slither like a snake?
Can you roar like a lion?
Can you jump like a dog?
Can you fly like a bat?
Can you meow like cat?
Can you caw like a rooster?
Can you?
Andrew Buck, Grade 1
Blessed Sacrament School, FL

Penguins
P enguins are cute
E xciting to see a penguin
N o other thing is cuter than a penguin
G lides over ice on their stomachs
U se their feet to carry egg
I like penguins very much
N ow in five years the young penguin
will find it's own mate
Mitchell Carl, Grade 3
McKinley Elementary School, PA

Fall Is Here!
I see pumpkins
I hear boo and I hear grrr!
I smell candy
I feel goo
I taste apples
Wren Castor, Grade 1
McKinley Elementary School, PA

Fall/Autumn
Fall
Pretty, colorful
Falling, raking, jumping
Trees turn bright colors.
Autumn
Heidi Johnson, Grade 3
Kane Area Elementary/Middle School, PA

High Merit Poems – Grades K, 1, 2, and 3

Thanksgiving Day
Sometimes on Thanksgiving Day
I like to play.
The leaves are on the ground.
Happiness is all around.
We will have fun
Until it is done.
Grace Schifferdecker, Grade 3
Helderberg Christian School, NY

Paper
I see kids crumbling, cutting,
ripping, writing, shredding and
playing with paper all day.
When they do that it sounds
like it is snowing, raining, and there
is lightning.
Gianluca Chiodi, Grade 3
Our Lady of Hope School, NY

Travis
T errific
R espectful
A wesome
V ery helpful
I nteresting
S o fascinating
Elvira Osegueda Ramos, Grade 3
Bensley Elementary School, VA

Snow
S urrounded by white
N o leaves on trees anymore
O n cold days it is fun to play
W e like to play
Moises Herrera, Grade 3
Northeast Elementary School, NY

Summer
Pools, beaches, water parks
Bathing suits, shorts, short sleeves
Vacation, no school, go away!
Gregorio Riga, Grade 2
Weston Elementary School, NJ

Brendan
I am yellow
I am sweet
I am yummy
I am cool
But I am not an apple
I am a banana
Brendan Rodriguez, Grade 1
Northeast Elementary School, NY

Horses
H orseback riding
O h so fun!
R elaxing
S tallion
E xercising
S addle
Sierra Bowman, Grade 3
Wapping Elementary School, CT

When Is Thanksgiving?
When, steaming, turkeys, roast
When, huge, parades, march
When, tender, potatoes, boil
When, juicy, apple cider, slushes
Then it's Thanksgiving
Dziekuje
Marty Piskorowski, Grade 3
Triangle Elementary School, NJ

The Fall
In the fall,
The trees are so tall.
When the birds sing,
It makes my ears ring.
Sal D'Angelo, Grade 3
Our Lady of Hope School, NY

Mom
My mom loves me.
On Sunday, she takes me to church.
My mom doesn't like pineapples.
Caleb Spinelli, Grade 1
St Stephen's School, NY

Things from My Heart

I love my pop-pop
I love my mom
I love my dad
and I love my
brother and my
sister. I love my
pop-pop
because
he makes me
happy. I love my
mom because
she makes me
smile. I love
my dad because
he loves me. I
love my brother
and sister because
they make me
smile a lot.

Dana Jackson, Grade 3
William M Meredith School, PA

A Perfect Pencil

I see a perfect pencil
I see it in the cup
I see it with my eye
I try to snatch it...

No luck!

This pencil I need!
Without it my words will be dull
I see the person with it...
Who I don't know

I step slowly, slow
"Students!," my teacher yells
"Got it!," I scream
Just another week in detention...

Caroline O'Donnell, Grade 3
Memorial School, NH

Peace Is...

Lovely
Holy
Family time
A trip to Los Angeles.
Reading the Bible.
A full moon.
Listening to the waves.
Sleeping in my bed.
But most of all,
Peace is a dove flying away.

Elijah Barnes, Grade 3
St Augustine Cathedral School, CT

Peace Is...

Loving people in my family.
Calm animals by the waterfall.
Quiet places like the country.
Wonderful mountains and valleys.
Relaxing on my comfy bed.
Having a good dream.
Going to beautiful places with my family.
Crickets chirping in the night.
But most of all,
Peace is knowing God is with me.

Michael Finn, Grade 3
St Augustine Cathedral School, CT

Peace Is...

Loving my family.
A sunset at night.
Caring for the world.
Reading a book.
Looking at a waterfall.
A quiet place.
Looking into the sky.
Smelling fresh air.
But most of all,
Peace is Nature.

Christina Marcellus, Grade 3
St Augustine Cathedral School, CT

High Merit Poems – Grades K, 1, 2, and 3

My Friend Hani

Sometimes I forgive my friend, Hani
Sometimes we fight
When we fight, I get mad
I forgive him because he is my friend
Hani makes me happy when we play video games together
We like to go to McDonald's and go to the play room

Ethan Estrada, Grade 1
New York Institute for Special Education, NY

I Love Her

I love my mom
She lets me go on the computer and
She always gives me hugs
My mom cooks for me
I hug and kiss my mom so she knows I love her
I am happy she is in my life because she takes me to stores

Dylinn Cruz, Grade 3
New York Institute for Special Education, NY

Autumn

The leaves being guided gracefully with the wind,
The crisp apples dangling from the mighty, tough trees,
The squirrels and chipmunks communicating,
The strong flavored and crisp apple pie on the tip of my tongue,
The refreshing air blowing against me,
And the crunchy leaves falling all over my body.

Ivana Klontz, Grade 2
Wellington School, FL

I Love Christmas

I love the sound of bells shaking…
bright, noisy gifts from Santa…
I love when Santa, "HO, HO, HOs!!!"
I love Christmas more than any other holiday.

Thomas Brodowski, Grade 2
St John the Apostle Catholic School, VA

Peacocks

Peacocks spread their feathers out high in the sky.
They fluff them up, and they are like a rainbow in the sky.
Peacocks barely fly.

Samantha Lin, Grade 3
Sweetwater Episcopal Academy, FL

Love

Roses are red
Violets are blue
No one is as sweet as you
You are smart in every way
I love seeing you every day
playing, running, jumping high
I just hate to say goodbye!

Mia Nieves, Grade 3
Number 12 Elementary School, NJ

Aaliyah

A doring family and teacher
A ble to jump from high bar into the pit
L istens to family
I n love with helping others
Y ay for sharing snacks with friends
A wesome at Wii Fit
H ooray! I bring smiles to all

Aaliyah Cotton, Grade 1
St John Neumann Academy, VA

New York City

When I'm in the mood to see my relatives,
I'll be shopping in New York City,
To hear the loud music,
To watch cars and people talking,
While I visit my grandma,
I'll be back again next month,
When I'm in the mood to see my relatives.

Nikolett Colon, Grade 3
Marie Curie Institute, NY

Sweet Tooth

I love brownies...

Mom and I lick the bowl
like little pigs.

We always have to share the batter
with my mean brother.

Ainsley Proctor, Grade 2
St John the Apostle Catholic School, VA

Kittens

K iss you
I tch their ears
T ake lick baths
T hey are furry
E at fish and mice
N ap with you
S cratch you

Hailey Duma, Grade 2
Marie Curie Institute, NY

My Pet Dog

My pet dog.
My dog goes scratch, scratch, scratch.
He jumps, jumps, jumps.
He rolls, rolls, rolls.
He barks, barks, barks.
He chomps, chomps, chomps, chomps.
My pet dog.

Kai Walls, Grade 2
Sweetwater Episcopal Academy, FL

Snow

Snowmen
Snow fights
Snow forts
Snow balls
Snow boots
Snow jackets
Snow

Megan Simko, Grade 2
Weston Elementary School, NJ

Thanksgiving

I love Thanksgiving
N ovember
D ay to celebrate
I give thanks
A pple pie
N ow it is time to eat
S tuffing

Madison Roman, Grade 1
St Agatha School, NY

High Merit Poems – Grades K, 1, 2, and 3

Baby
B aby crying
A lways sleeping
B aby drooling
Y oung child
Luzmari Torres, Grade 2
Marie Curie Institute, NY

Birds and Kids
Birds are singing tweet, tweet, tweet.
Kids are playing yay, yay, yay.
Birds love singing all year round.
Kids love playing every day.
Julia Gravagna, Grade 3
Our Lady of Hope School, NY

Christmas Fun
Every snowy day the kids
will say hurray!
The presents will start to come
for every single one.
Jenna Muro, Grade 3
Our Lady of Hope School, NY

At the Barn
As the wind blows through the wheat field
And as the horse trots,
It seems like they are together
Joyfully singing a song
Joseph MacDonough, Grade 3
St Raphael School, MD

This Is Christmas
Santa is coming
Mrs. Claus is waiting
The elves are loving
People are singing
Renée Crowe, Grade 3
Our Lady of Hope School, NY

Love
L ove is a special thing
O ur family is full of love
V ery strong feelings
E veryone is loved in a different way
Kiyah Harris, Grade 3
Bensley Elementary School, VA

The Snow
The snow is blowing, roaring, soaring.
It sounds like it is talking.
It is covering the houses,
and it is looking so beautiful.
Jessie Biondo, Grade 3
Our Lady of Hope School, NY

Cats
Sleeping, playing, purring
Scratching, hiding, climbing
Licking, jumping, rolling
Cats
David Fabiyan, Grade 2
Weston Elementary School, NJ

The Penguins
The penguins are gliding.
Now they are sliding.
They are flipping.
Now they are searching for food.
Emmanuela Panepinto, Grade 3
Our Lady of Hope School, NY

Love
L ove is in the air
O h, what a great feeling
V alentine's Day
E veryone should feel loved
Chrysta Gray, Grade 3
Bensley Elementary School, VA

Thanksgiving

My life as a Pilgrim
On the Mayflower
It was hard
We could hardly sleep on the ship
There were a lot of storms
It made me sick
When we landed at Plymouth
We found plants to cook
We played games and made houses
We had a lot to do
I had lots of fun with the Wampanoag
They were nice
We found lots of cool rocks and shells on the sea
To a Pilgrim
Thanksgiving is the best holiday

Elizabeth Perillo, Grade 3
St Mary School, NY

Halloween Night

As I was walking down the street
I saw a pumpkin fat and neat
Oh what a treat!
The yummy pumpkin seeds
Then my pumpkin begins to speed
Next a wild cat stops my pumpkin
And an invisible ghost makes a grin
His tail got burned in a cauldron
He decided to call 9-1-1
9-1-1 was a group of vampires
Who saw a ghost was burnt on fire!
They sprayed water on the ghost
Who looked like a piece of toast
Then they all disappeared into the night sky
That was the end of Halloween night. Bye, Bye!

Sarah Molnarova, Grade 2
Wellington School, FL

Trains

Trains carry coal and they drive on the tracks.
They work from day to night, they are fun.
I am going to ride a train

Christopher M. Kaatz, Grade 1
St John Neumann Academy, VA

High Merit Poems – Grades K, 1, 2, and 3

Indians
I mportant
N ative Americans
D eer skin
I love them
A merican
N ice
S quanto
Jacob Mello, Grade 3
Wapping Elementary School, CT

Camping
C amper
A n adventure
M aking s'mores
P utting up a tent
I love camping
N ever-ending fun
G athering wood for the fire
Carlyn Burba, Grade 3
Wapping Elementary School, CT

Moon into Sun
Moon
Silver, different, shaped
Shining, sparkling, brightening
Beautiful, sky, clouds, hot
Beaming, steaming, gleaming
Bright, light
Sun
Nadia Huebner, Grade 3
Ross Elementary School, PA

Lava to Water
Lava
Hot, red
Flaming, heating, blazing
Volcano, Hawaii, ice, frost
Running, splashing, freezing
Cool, beautiful
Water
Jesse Crownover, Grade 3
Ross Elementary School, PA

Shark/Dolphin
Shark
Ferocious, aggressive
Terrifying, attacking, tearing
Orca, crocodile, graceful, gorgeous
Flipping, swimming, loving
Pretty, talented
Dolphin
Megan Wurster, Grade 3
Ross Elementary School, PA

Reptiles to Mammal
Reptiles
Scaly, bumpy
Crawling, slithering, hiding
Icky, dirty, soft, furry
Swallowing, nibbling, chewing
Belly button, happy
Mammal
Ana Gongloff, Grade 3
Ross Elementary School, PA

Pizza to Peppers
Pizza
Hot, red
Baking, cutting, eating
Cheese, crust, vine, red
Growing, eating, cooking
Spicy, hot
Peppers
Julian Drake, Grade 1
Ross Elementary School, PA

Cat to Dog
Cat
Fluffy, cute
Purring, scratching, running
Fur, claw, bark, paws
Licking, crawling, barking
Soft, lovable
Dog
Maggie Knox, Grade 1
Ross Elementary School, PA

Teachers

T eachers teach kids
E ach teacher has rules
A teacher can put you in time out
C an't talk while the teacher is talking
H ave all materials ready
E ach student needs to pay attention
R egrouping is what we're learning in Math
S tay on point in Ms. Griffin's class

Ilyus Gomez, Grade 3
Bensley Elementary School, VA

Ghosts

G hastly ghosts
H unt in the spooky country
O ver the tall mountain where the werewolves howl. In the middle of the
S pooky country. There is a foggy graveyard, and the white ghosts come up
T o scare your pants off. They say, "Have a
S pooktacular night!"

Luke Pepin, Grade 2
Consolidated School, CT

Costumes

C amouflage spooky costumes
O n a frisky night.
S ay TRICK-OR-TREAT
T o creepy strangers
U nknown to me.
M ysterious?
E at all the candy you can!!
S uddenly a screech filled the air. I fainted!

Lexi Nunnally, Grade 2
Consolidated School, CT

My Mom and Dad

I love my mom because
she cooks for me and my family. I love my dad
because he works for my family, too. My mom and dad
love me. We are a great big
family!

Leah Cruz, Grade 1
Mother Seton Inter Parochial School, NJ

Fireballs on Friday

As I was falling asleep in my hammock,
I began dreaming of rainbows and unicorns.
Then suddenly I began to panic.
It seemed like the BFG blew a trogglehumper through his horn.

The beautiful rainbows disappeared.
Then came a big, scary creature,
Bald, with a very long beard
And displaying very ugly features.

The creature chased my brother and me,
Shooting fireballs from his mouth.
I freaked out and fainted and Thomas could see
He needed to help, so we headed South.

Into the house we flew like a bee,
But the giant picked up the roof.
The house was destroyed so we sprinted for a tree,
And hoped this tree was giant-proof.

On his way the giant tripped on a log
And landed head first in a pool.
Suddenly I woke up in a fog
And I thought to myself, "That nightmare was pretty cool!"

Laura Lampognana, Grade 3
Infant Jesus School, NH

Hot Chocolate

H ot drinks in the winter.
O ne snow flake fell on the roof.
T he snowflakes begin to come into my face.

C ars are covered with snow.
H ot warm clothes in the winter.
O ne big pile of snow.
C an be so much fun.
O h it tastes so yummy.
L et's have it after we go out in the cold.
A super treat.
T astes great with whip cream.
E veryone should have a cup.

Jeffrey Abad, Grade 3
Northeast Elementary School, NY

It Was a Dark and Stormy Night
It was a dark and stormy night, the clouds were low, the sky was gray
A single raindrop fell on the last speck of light as it faded away
Eight more raindrops fell
Eighty more raindrops fell
Eight hundred more raindrops fell
Eight thousand more raindrops fell
The rain pitter-pattered on the roof
A flash of lightning streaked across the sky — Boom!
Another flash of lightning shattered the sky and lit up the night
Then blackness filled the night
The only light left was from the wood fire in the fireplace as it slowly burned down
    to nothing.

Carson Gaines, Grade 3
George Hersey Robertson Intermediate School, CT

The Sea of Sleep
The sea of sleep
Is as blue as the night sky As her quiet ripples tiptoe on the shore
Slippery, sly, sky high
Dreamy dolphins dive and dip in a deep, blue jewel
Brilliant crystals gleam and glint
Gleam and glint
The sea of sleep Cradles the coral
In its silver waves
So big and bright
The sea of sleep
Moves along
Over many and many a million years

Grace Vest, Grade 3
Jeffrey Elementary School, CT

Christmas
C ase of big presents
H old big present that you want to play with
R ip up all the bags
I like to get good presents
S ave all the good toys you like
T oys everywhere from Santa
M ake good things for your family
A present from your mom and dad
S ee a gift that is fun and play with it

Brandon Yanez, Grade 3
Northeast Elementary School, NY

Halloween Night

Halloween Night comes once a year
Witches, goblins and ghosts appear.
Mummies and vampires walk the streets
Going house to house for lots of treats.

Pumpkins with their faces that glow
What's around the bend, we may never know
The leaves blow in the cool night air
Be the first to the door, if you dare.

Trick of Treat we say over and over
Everyone's in a costume, even Rover
My costume is hot and up to my ears
But it will be worth it for the 3 Musketeers

The full moon rises over the trees
My friend fell over and scraped his knee
We are done with the houses on my street
Now it's time to race home with candy to eat.

Michael Schneider, Grade 3
St Alexis School, PA

The Giant Dream

There once was a boy named Lee who was treated with good care.
But, one night he had a giant nightmare.
He dreamed that there was a mean giant named Doug
Who hurt little kids with his powerful tug.
One day this cruel, ugly giant took Lee
To work for him without a fee.
Lee did what Doug said right away
In fear to be thrown in the bay.
He worked for ten days and nights
And he tried to please Doug with all his might.
After twenty horrible, bad, dirty days,
Lee decided to run far far away.
He knew when he was found by Doug
He would be cooked in his special red mug.
When the real Lee woke up
He was twisting like a scared pup.
Lee knew it was a dream
Because there was no such thing as a giant that was mean!

Elizabeth Ross, Grade 3
Infant Jesus School, NH

Imagination

Your imagination can take you to places.
Your imagination can take you to a plane, car or even outer space.
Your imagination can take you to places beyond your dreams.
Your imagination is something you can be or do.
Whatever you desire to do it is up to you.

It is up to you to let your imagination run wild.
You can be whoever you want to be.
And experience whatever your heart leads you to.
You can travel the world at the speed of lightning.
Your imagination will say come along for the ride.
Have the best imagination of your life.

Naselin Mendez, Grade 3
Public School 131, NY

First Grade

F irst day — I wasn't very calm.
I really, really missed my Mom.
R unning the playground in the sun,
S chool then started to be lots of fun.
T eacher couldn't wait to teach;

G reat books were everywhere you could reach.
R eading them is very cool!
A rule at school: don't be a fool.
" **D** arling," Mom asked, "was school okay?"
" **E** xcellent Day!" she heard me say.

Susanna Harnish, Grade 1
The American Academy, PA

Books Are Awesome!

I think books are the most wonderful things in the world, world, world!
They're soooo good, good, good.
They're so interesting, interesting, interesting.
I like adventure, adventure, adventure,
And mystery, mystery, mystery.
I think you should try to read some.
You sure would like them, them, them.
They're fun to read, interesting,
And you'll get smart, smart, smart.
That's why I think you should read books, books, books!

Dominique Gabrielle Scerbak, Grade 3
St Mary's School, NJ

High Merit Poems – Grades K, 1, 2, and 3

I Promote Peace
If there is
a lot of noise
in school,
I help to make peace
by reminding the kids
to be quiet.
If you're reading
a book
this can help you.
Kameron Poupis, Grade 1
Our Lady of Mercy Regional School, NY

Christmas
On Christmas day
everybody is going to play
with all their new toys.
The bells on Santa's deer
might hurt some people's ears.
While the elves are making toys
people might make noise.
People also start playing,
cooking and snow sleighing.
Gio Miceli, Grade 3
Our Lady of Hope School, NY

Christmas
C hristmas presents
H aving fun in the snow
R eally pretty wreath decorations
I ce cream for dessert
S now all over the place
T ying ribbons on presents
M ass
A sking for cake
S tuck in the snow
Mairin McDonnell, Grade 3
McKinley Elementary School, PA

Christmas
C arolers
H olidays
R espect for others
I love to be jolly
S top being snotty
T ons of snow falling
M aking snowballs
A lot of presents
S anta
Jonathan Noe, Grade 3
Northeast Elementary School, NY

Fall Is Here!
I see graves
I hear trick or treaters
I smell candy
I feel my Halloween costume
I taste apple cider
Brian Courduff, Grade 1
McKinley Elementary School, PA

Thanksgiving
Thanksgiving
Turkey, dinner
Tasting, smelling, thrilling
Thanksgiving turkey smelling good
Turkey
Lasha Gonzalez, Grade 3
Marie Curie Institute, NY

Maine Winter
Firewood
snow plow
snow angels disappear
lively flutter
dead bushes
my hat missing.
Rowan Collins, Grade 2
Fairfield Elementary School, ME

My Friends
I like my friends because
we play a lot. I love my
friends, who care, and they
are so smart.
My friends are cool and
we like to play at school.
Jasmine Flores, Grade 1
Mother Seton Inter Parochial School, NJ

Can You?

Can you run like a dog?
Can you scratch like a cat?
Can you hop like a bunny?
Can you squeak like a mouse?
Can you slide on your belly like a penguin?
Can you fly like a love bug?
Can you stay as still as a turtle?
As still as that?
Can you?

Abigail Lawless, Grade 1
Blessed Sacrament School, FL

The Butterfly Flies Away

B eautiful
U nder the flowers
T apping its wings
T ogether making a song of the garden
E very flight is a joy to watch in the sky
R emembering a time of fun and excitement
F lutter away butterfly
L et your journey be a happy one
Y ou are in my memory

Katie Hanline, Grade 1
St John Neumann Academy, VA

Living in the Ocean

When you go in the ocean you think it is fun
But when a shark is trying to bite you
It is not so fun!
Living in the ocean could be fun if you have a submarine
Especially at night
If you ever go in the ocean watch out for sharks!

Natalie Geoghegan, Grade 1
Richard E Byrd Elementary School, NJ

Germs

Germs, Germs – They are everywhere –
On your body and in your hair
They're something you should not share
These little creatures do not have a care
If they make you sick, it can be a nightmare!

Gianna D'Alessandro, Grade 2
Westtown Thornbury Elementary School, PA

High Merit Poems – Grades K, 1, 2, and 3

The Color of Spring
Outside the color changes.
Green, yellow, blue and orange
It rains to make the flowers grow
Petals as soft as caterpillar fur
The sun rises to help us see...
Flowers, butterflies, birds and ladybugs.
Amethyst Martin, Grade 2
Carlyle C Ring Elementary School, NY

Oh Baby Bottles!
Oh baby bottles, you squirt out fun.
Don't leave, it has just begun.
Red, Blue, Orange, and Green.
Baby bottles are extreme.
You can refill, open and close it.
You help babies drink not from the sink.
Ilayda Guneren, Grade 3
Bowne Munro Elementary School, NJ

Soccer
S oft kicks
O utstanding goals
C reative moves
C reative soccer balls
E merging fouls
R unning faster
Ceili'-Ann Courduff, Grade 3
McKinley Elementary School, PA

Fall and Autumn
Fall is autumn
And autumn is fall.
I like fall.
Autumn and fall are special.
In fall the leaves are red.
In fall I pick up red leaves.
Alan Li, Grade 2
Children's Village, PA

Eric
E xciting
R eally smart
I ndependent
C aring
Eric Duong, Grade 3
Bensley Elementary School, VA

The Zoo
Once I went to the zoo
There were lions, tigers and alligators too
I saw a peacock that was blue
The panda bears were eating bamboo!
Ryan Kilby, Grade 2
Mary Walter Elementary School, VA

A Friend
A friend a friend
We like a friend
A friend a friend
A friend makes me happy!
Kyle McGuinness Getzinger, Kindergarten
Middle Gate Elementary School, CT

The Colors of Art
Rainbows with lots of colors
are beautiful to draw.
To make it very pretty
I draw it all myself.
Cydney Amenda, Grade 1
Windsor Learning Academy, FL

Soccer
Balls, goalies, cleats
Free kick, penalty goal, score
Defense, forward, midfield
Soccer
Adam Berrocal, Grade 2
Weston Elementary School, NJ

Page 73

Winter

Snow comes
We make snowballs
So cold it gives me brain freeze
Come inside and make hot cocoa
Get your tummy warm!
Desiree Barr, Grade 2
Carlyle C Ring Elementary School, NY

Thanksgiving

F amily
E verybody celebrates
A pple pie
S tuffing
T urkey
Aidan Fechter, Grade 1
St Agatha School, NY

Gold

Gold is the color of trophies.
Gold is the color of awards.
If you are number one, you get gold.
If you are the champions, you get gold.
Go gold, go.
Jacob Lowe, Grade 2
Sweetwater Episcopal Academy, FL

Emily

E xcellent
M usical
I ndependent
L ovely
Y oung
Emily Knisely-Durham, Grade 3
McKinley Elementary School, PA

Ball

Ball
rubbery, weird
rough, soft, smooth
round, colorful, bouncing, rolling
throw, roll, catch, kick, score
Jason Gonzalez, Grade 2
Marie Curie Institute, NY

Pink

Pink is the color of a dress.
Pink is the color for a ribbon.
Pink is the color of mom's lipstick.
Pink is my bubble gum.
Yum, Yum!
Grace Klingman, Grade 2
Sweetwater Episcopal Academy, FL

Cat

Cat
hairy, dirty
soft, rough, furry
fur, ears, tail, claws
walks, sits, runs, meows, purrs
Alinah Marinov, Grade 2
Marie Curie Institute, NY

Dogs

Dogs
dirty, clean
furry, dry, soft
animal, fur, nose, paws
run, play, swim, sleep, growl
Gabriel Wheeler, Grade 2
Marie Curie Institute, NY

Can You?

Can you hop like a frog?
Can you waddle like a penguin?
Can you roar like a lion?
Can you slither like a snake?
Can you?
Victoria Ramella, Grade 1
Blessed Sacrament School, FL

Christmas

The bells are ringing,
the people are singing,
kids are enjoying opening their presents
Jesus is coming
and everyone is celebrating that day.
Matthew Yuen, Grade 3
Our Lady of Hope School, NY

Cape May, NJ

C urly, pink seaweed lay on the soft sandy beach,
A nd the glittering sun shone on the crashing waves.
P layful, leaping dolphins swam in the cold blue water.
E ndless beach lay before a calm ocean.

M ollusks and spiral shells settled at the ocean's edge.
A nd a camouflaged crab scuttled sideways through the sand.
Y ellow goldenrod attracted graceful monarch butterflies.

N o vacation is quite so great;
J ust jump in the ocean and take the bait.

Seth DeWitt, Grade 2
The American Academy, PA

Halloween

Skeletons rattling like marbles going down a tube,
Making me feel like an ice cube!
Witches making a bloody, crimson brew,
That's true!
Ghosts booing and rising from the city sewers
And dancing beautifully,
Witches cackling and flying by the crescent moon,
Goblins cooking up a lovely stew,
Bats humming in the clear night sky
That is so very clear!
I get a great big scare!!!

Dalton Hoch, Grade 2
Wellington School, FL

The Earth

The wonderful, wonderful earth.
Such lovely things from it bursts,
from the most beautiful creek to the toad that just spoke.
I saw a flying kite, it blew in the wind with all its might.
On the ground, animals feet made a big, big sound.
The bumblebee went to the apple tree to see the blossoms.
Scurrying across the road were two possums.
The white-tailed deer ran through the meadow.
The daisies were big, bright and yellow.
I think I should close my mouth and take a rest.
All I have to say now is..."Earth is the Best."

Kiaya James, Grade 3
Georgetown Elementary School, DE

A Celebration of Poets – East Grades K-3 Fall 2010

Presents
fun
birthday, Christmas
exciting, opening, surprising
open a new toy
gifts
Vanessa Santiago, Grade 3
Marie Curie Institute, NY

Dragons
Dragons soar through the night;
Flying the sky higher and higher,
The moon is so bright.
He stops to carefully land on the ground.
So he can rest on the rock he found.
Sara Skipper, Grade 3
Sweetwater Episcopal Academy, FL

Recycle
Recycle
Helping, living,
Reusing, recycling, reducing
Take care of earth
No littering
Destiny Rivera, Grade 3
Marie Curie Institute, NY

Horses
Horses are fast.
Horses are very pretty.
They are my favorite animal.
They are nice.
I like horses.
Gabriella Gray, Grade 3
Eagle's View Academy, FL

Football
Punting, touchdown, field goal
Fumble, intercepted, time out
Running back, quarterback, line receiver
Tackle, blind side, 2 point conversion
Football
Matthew Kussman, Grade 2
Weston Elementary School, NJ

Me
J anuary
A wesome
C ool
O lder
B rother
Jacob Koehler, Kindergarten
Sweetwater Episcopal Academy, FL

Cat
Cat
grass dirt
soft fluffy hairy
pretty white beautiful gray
meows walks jumps hisses growls
Alex Slovack, Grade 2
Marie Curie Institute, NY

Tiger
Tiger
stinky dirty
soft meat furry
orange black white stripes
moves loud runs jumps growls
Zowie Zabielski, Grade 2
Marie Curie Institute, NY

Ghost
G houls
H aunted house
O ctober
S cary
T reats
Matthew Curran, Grade 3
McKinley Elementary School, PA

Mariah
I am
pretty, fast as fast can be
good at sports, awesome on all the courts
talkative, good at reading, and smart
3 2 1 jump ball let's start
Mariah Cheek, Grade 3
Number 12 Elementary School, NJ

High Merit Poems – Grades K, 1, 2, and 3

My Day at the Beach

One day at the beach as I swam in the ocean,
I glanced upon a shell that seemed to be in motion.

It moved so slowly but didn't seem to have any feet,
It glided and danced to a different beat.

Its antennas swayed from side to side,
I touched its shell it seemed to hide

It tucked itself inside because it was afraid,
I quickly learned what a mistake I had made.

I put it back down and waited to see
If he would move again if I let him be.

He came out of his shell and glided toward me,
What a beautiful creature so innocent and free.

I hope when I come back soon someday,
I will pray to see my new friend if there is any way.

Michael Arndt, Grade 3
Windsor Learning Academy, FL

The Tree Project

There once was a girl named Kyla
Who researched a Ficus Carica
She had such a blast
Couldn't wait to share with her class
For her project she hoped they'd admire.

She hopped over the fence to observe
For a grade she probably deserve
She doesn't eat pigs
But she devoured those figs
For her hunger she did not curve.

Mrs. Moerler this adventure was fun
From since the time that it had begun
The things I now know
So much pictures to show
And now my poem is done.

Kyla James, Grade 2
Public School 235 Janice Marie Knight, NY

Family

The people around me who I love and that care for me are my family. My brother is who I look up to. My sister who helps me when I'm in need. My father who I love is the best. The cousins I have are fun to be around. Aunts and uncles are like my parents, when my mom and dad aren't around. My mom is the most important of them all, who I care for when she is sick. The lady who I love and will always love. This is my family, who I think is the best in the world

Justin Paguirigan, Grade 3
Number 12 Elementary School, NJ

The Gingerbread Cookie

Gingerbread cookies are fragile, crisp men with candy eyes.
Crunch! That great taste.
The cookies are very cinnamony and gingery.
They smell like ginger.
Their brown bodies are very yummy to taste.
They are very scrumptious once you take one bite.

Connor McGee, Grade 3
Riverton Public School, NJ

I Love My Teachers

I love my teachers
They teach me well and care about me.
I appreciate them and feel lucky to have them.
They do things for me.
They care about me.
I love them.

Almasi Johnson, Grade 3
New York Institute for Special Education, NY

Cell

C ells are cool
E lephants have lots of cells
L ions have a bunch of cells
L ot of cells in a body

Zachary Chisek, Grade 3
Susquehanna Community Elementary School, PA

Dreamer

No dreamer is ever too big. No dreamer is ever too small.
Dream big, dream small but always dream your dreams!
Be a dreamer and all your dreams will come true.

Julia Preston, Grade 2
Sol Feinstone Elementary School, PA

High Merit Poems – Grades K, 1, 2, and 3

The World Is Forever
The world is forever
My heart will be forever
My eyes— forever, forever, forever
I'll have my ears
I'll have my head
Forever and forever
I'll have my feet, too
I will have God watching me
Forever and ever
I'll have my fingers
Forever and ever
Forever
Jessie Robie, Grade 2
Clover Street School, CT

The Peaceful Sea
The fish are swimming peacefully
The dolphins are jumping high in the air
The sea is calm and clear tonight
The waves are bumping around
And the moon lights the way
The beach is empty
Nobody is out tonight
It is very beautiful tonight
The fish are sleeping
The otters are floating calmly
The dolphins have stopped jumping
The animals are sleeping tonight.
Jonathan Mader, Grade 3
Jeffrey Elementary School, CT

Thanksgiving
M y family celebrates Thanksgiving
A lot of turkeys trying to stay alive
Y um, turkeys baking
F amily feast
L ots of people having fun
O ctober is gone, but November is here
W e give thanks
E veryone eating different foods
R eady to eat turkey
Gabriel Samolyuk, Grade 3
St Agatha School, NY

Scared of Storms
I am at home,
and I am lonely.
I am freezing like a statue.
Daylight falls.
Thunder is coming.
Lightning is striking.
Both are crashing each other.
Ka-Boom!
Lightning zaps trees into splits.
I go up to my bedroom.
I close the door,
and put my pillow on top of my head.
I fell asleep in my happy dreams.
Yajat Bungatavula, Grade 3
Oak Ridge Elementary School, PA

Swimming
Swimming is my sport,
I am the best at backstroke.
Some swimmers are short,
if you watch me swim I am no joke.
My friends say I am like a fish,
I have a lot of swim caps.
It would be my wish,
to swim eight laps.
It is fun to win,
because I am fast.
I feel like I have a fin,
because I go right past.
Meghan Boyczuk, Grade 3
Ellicott Road Elementary School, NY

Football
Touchdown!
Do a dance
Run the ball!
Wind in my face
Tackle!
Strong and powerful
Football
Eat, sleep, breathe.
Cole Simmons, Grade 2
Carlyle C Ring Elementary School, NY

December
D ancing ballerinas
E ating food
C hristmas presents
E xciting for my family
M y mom's birthday
B aking a Christmas cake
E ating eggs and bacon
R eading Christmas cards
Rebecca Iracheta, Grade 3
Bensley Elementary School, VA

Fall
Fall is cool.
All leaves
Blow in the breeze.
I raked leaves of red
In a bed.
Fall is tall.
That's why I like fall.
Erik Koivu, Grade 2
Eagle's View Academy, FL

Flowers
Flowers, flowers in a vase.
How many are there?
Six or eight?
Some are red
Some are blue
Flowers, flowers...
I love you!
Sara Ladhani, Grade 3
Sweetwater Episcopal Academy, FL

Reading
I like to read
My book The Cake
Falls on My Dog's Head
It's so funny
It makes me laugh
And read some more
Today at school
Kelin Levya, Kindergarten
Windsor Learning Academy, FL

I Can Promote Peace
I n small ways...I can promote peace...

C ompassion
A lways ready to forgive
N ice words

P oliteness
R espect
O rdinary wisdom
M ercy
O utstanding justice
T ake time to listen
E quality and fairness

P ractice and patience
E mpathy
A cts of kindness
C harity
E mbrace love
Matthew W. Naugles, Grade 2
Our Lady of Mercy Regional School, NY

Peace
Peace is a bird
flying through the air
Peace is a man
talking to his friend
Peace is a plant
standing in the sun
Peace is a teacher
helping her students
Peace is a butterfly
sipping nectar from a flower
Peace is a caterpillar
climbing through the trees
Peace is a frog
hopping around
Peace is a fish
bubbling underwater
Peace is a dog
running after a frisbee
Christopher Meade, Grade 3
William M Meredith School, PA

High Merit Poems – Grades K, 1, 2, and 3

Rain
rain goes down fast
and then you hear
rain go splish, splash
like a baby crying with
watery tears all
over the place
Yosi Kearney, Grade 3
William M Meredith School, PA

When Is Thanksgiving?
When colorful leaves fall
When a big family eats
When creamy apple pie is sliced
When messy hot cocoa spills
Then it's Thanksgiving!
Grazie!
Julianna Yarka, Grade 3

Buses
Buses
dirty, clean
smooth, metal, hard
yellow, silver, black, white
drop-off, pickup, beep, roll, bump
Zachary Wilson, Grade 2
Marie Curie Institute, NY

Cows
C ows on wheels
O ff road
W atch them go!
S elling seeds
Benny Silva, Grade 3
Wapping Elementary School, CT

A Hot Day
Steaming summer day,
Swimming in a nice cool pool,
Oh what a hot day!
Zachary Heske, Grade 2
St Mary's School, NJ

When Is Thanksgiving?
When helpful Indians hunt
When thick pumpkin pie rises
When cold Pilgrims pray
When juicy ham leaks
Then it's Thanksgiving!
Danke!
Luke Monsorno, Grade 3
Triangle Elementary School, NJ

Autumn
A pples are sweet and crunchy
U nder the tree were leaves
T hanksgiving comes near Halloween
U se an umbrella to keep dry
M y mom makes turkey
N o, I don't like stuffing
Ashli Malvita, Grade 3
Central Park Elementary School, FL

Autumn
A ll turkeys are
U seful to
T hanksgiving dinner
U se pumpkin pie and
M unchie foods but
N ever eat pancakes on Thanksgiving!
Jacquelynn Lovegren, Grade 3
Central Park Elementary School, FL

Pillow Fights
Laughing, giggling, smiling
Full of foam, full of feathers
Wildly swinging
Wham!
Hannah Mikol, Grade 3
Memorial School, NH

My Mom
My mom is running.
Oh how she likes to swim.
My mom is walking.
Marissa Mistriner, Grade 1
St Stephen's School, NY

Fall Is Here!
I see zombies
I hear a ghost saying boo!
I smell apples
I feel grave stones
I taste pumpkin seeds
William Pickering, Grade 1
McKinley Elementary School, PA

Fall Is Here!
I see Frankenstein
I hear ghosts saying boo!
I smell apple pie
I feel goo
I taste candy
Lannen Lare, Grade 1
McKinley Elementary School, PA

Candy/Sweets
Candy
Sweet, sugary
Unwrapping, eating, stuffing
Sweet candy is good!
Sweets
Dominic O'Rourke, Grade 3
Kane Area Elementary/Middle School, PA

Monsters/Creatures
Monsters
Scary, slimy
Sneaking, hiding, scaring
They are fairy tales.
Creatures
Blake Ebeling, Grade 3
Kane Area Elementary/Middle School, PA

Fall Is Here!
I see trees swaying
I hear squeaking bats
I smell yummy turkey
I feel lots of wind
I taste apple cake
Myles Winegrad, Grade 1
McKinley Elementary School, PA

Summers End
See ya Hershey Park
Big, brown, chocolatey, Hershey guy
Nice, flat, wide, big screen TV
Fast, spinning Tilt A Whirl

So long Seaside Heights
sandy, hot beach
big, high boardwalk rides
small, comfy condo

Later Swim Team
encouraging coaches
1st place ribbons
warm, deep pool

Farewell Seaside Waterpark
yummy, cinnamon churros
warm, bubbly, hot tub
crazy, slippery, jungle gym

Goodbye summer. Looking forward
to seeing you next year!
James Kendra, Grade 3
Liberty School, NJ

Summer Vacation
S unny
U nder a tree at home
M issing school
M y trip to Canada
E xciting part of the year
R elaxing

V ery nice season
A t least I don't have homework
C ousin's pool
A t home
T V
I can rest
O ff for two and a half months
N ice to go outside
Emil Mathew, Grade 3
Wapping Elementary School, CT

The Sky

The sky,
looks like
a river
in the air
in the
afternoon

When it sets,
It looks like
a giant
pencil eraser
and fire burning

At night,
it looks like
the leftover
dark damp coal
and there are
leftover sparks
From when the fire
was burning.

Lang Le, Grade 1
Latimer Lane School, CT

The Sea of Sleep

Only the sand remembers
People slightly stepping on the sand
Dreamy dolphins
Swiftly glide through the water
Miniature sea stars
Slowly sway their snakelike arms
Over many and many a million years
Only the water remembers
The fishing boats
Softly gliding through the water
Barnacles bouncing
In the silver waves looking for a dock
Driftwood dances
Through the water likes a whirlpool
Over many and many a million years
Water

Malone Krouch, Grade 3
Jeffrey Elementary School, CT

Christmas

C heerful, fun, creative too
H appy time for me and you
R ighteousness for all to learn
I magination and love is due
S tars are there on the special night
T insel is hung at every sight
M orning time has just begun
A good time to sing the blues
S anta comes and gives us joy

Stockings hung and filled with fun.

Olivia Foster, Grade 3
Sweetwater Episcopal Academy, FL

A Great Christmas Treat

We take the cookie right out of the oven,
And smell that gingery spice.
He looks so good.
Time to decorate!
White icing for the mouth and nose,
With gumdrop buttons.
Time to eat!
I take the first bite,
I can taste that gingery spice.
Yummy!
What a Christmas treat!

Emily Myers, Grade 3
Riverton Public School, NJ

My Best Friend Ashton

Ashton likes **A** pples

Ashton does not like to **S** leep

Ashton has a fun **H** ouse

Ashton likes to watch **T** V

Ashton likes to eat **O** ranges

Ashton plays with **N** injas

Raj Vadodaria, Kindergarten
Pine Road Elementary School, PA

A Celebration of Poets – East Grades K-3 Fall 2010

Halloween Night

Oh how I love Halloween Night
Witches and goblins are such a fright
When it gets dark, out come the bats
Swooping overhead of the cats and rats

My brother and I dress in our Star Wars costumes
We carried light sabers, not witches' brooms
The night was cold, but our bodies were not
We took off with friends so we could not be caught

Kids love to yell 'trick or treat'
Collecting candy is really neat
We eat candy until we are sick
Our tummies start aching really quick

Werewolves and vampires are such a scare
Turn around please and be aware
I can't wait for next year; it's such a good time
I'll have a new costume and a new rhyme

Abigail Birch, Grade 3
St Alexis School, PA

How I Promote Peace

In your heart, something lies
a speck of dust! is its size.
Happiness and peace always rise.

Sometimes my sisters and I disagree,
but in the end it is always us three.

Sometimes friends don't play fair,
but in the end I know they care.

My older sister thinks we're in the way,
but at the end of the day we always play.

I'm happy in my heart.
If everyone else was too, wars would not start!

Riley Madigan, Grade 3
Our Lady of Mercy Regional School, NY

Every Window Needs a Cat

You know every window needs a cat,
Everybody knows that.
Peaceful, purring, softly snoring, little cats.

Little cats run and play,
But then it's time to sleep today.
Watching birds flying past, every window needs a cat.

By the window, time to rest,
Watching birds build their nests.
Tired little beauty cats.

Safe and fast good nights past,
Orange, black, red or white,
Sleepy cats say good night.

Meow, meow, one by one,
Little kittens sleeping fun.
Sleepy, sleepy window cats.

Sarah Hosking, Grade 2
Northampton Borough Elementary School, PA

The Colors: Red, Blue, Green

Red is a pretty color.
It is the color of a cherry.
It is the color of my heart.
It is the color of a ruby which is a precious stone.

Blue is a special color.
It is the color of the sky.
It is the color of my pencil case lying on the table.
It is the color of my classroom bulletin board.
It is the color of my ball.

Green is an amazing color.
It is the color of a green forest.
It is the color of a tree in the spring.
It is the color of a lizard crawling on a tree.
Green is the color of the grass near the tree.

Red, blue, and green are all pretty colors.

Jonathan Shek, Grade 3
Public School 131, NY

Cleanup

I cleaned my room
It was a mess
My animal and my dolls
Were everywhere
Mom was upset
So I did my best

Soledad Allen, Kindergarten
Windsor Learning Academy, FL

Hearts

Hearts are big and red
I give them to my mom
On every special day
Even on Disney days
To say thank you
And I love you

Anthony Cassille, Kindergarten
Windsor Learning Academy, FL

Walking My Dog

I want to walk my dog
she likes to look around.
She really gets excited
digging holes in the ground.
She likes to meet other dogs
because she really likes to play.

Kennedy McCloud, Grade 2
Windsor Learning Academy, FL

Thanksgiving

G ive thanks
O range colors
B rown colors
B ig celebration
L ots of Turkey
E verybody likes Thanksgiving

Mya Neciunas-Atwell, Grade 1
St Agatha School, NY

When Is Thanksgiving?

When lovable Grandpa talks
When huge parades march
When thick turkeys roast
When crumpling leaves pop
Then it's Thanksgiving
Grazie!

Kelly Riggs, Grade 3
Triangle Elementary School, NJ

When Is Thanksgiving?

When delicious potatoes are eaten
When juicy ham roasts
When humongous feasts get devoured
When excited Nick eats turkey
Then it's Thanksgiving!
Spasibo!

Nick Dooley, Grade 3
Triangle Elementary School, NJ

When Is Thanksgiving?

When loud turkeys gobble.
When sweet potatoes are mashed.
When fluffy rolls are buttered.
When huge parades march.
Then it's Thanksgiving!
Gracias!

Liam McGann, Grade 3
Triangle Elementary School, NJ

Autumn

A corns fall from trees
U nbelievable pumpkins
T he trees are different colors
U se the rake when the leaves fall
M ore leaves are falling down
N ovember is when fall starts

Jada Scott, Grade 3
Bensley Elementary School, VA

Halloween

Wind whistled
whooshing past my ears
leaves whistling in the dark
waiting for it to stop
ghosts out
goblins out
haunting a castle
it was Halloween
Nicholas Drown, Grade 2
Dyer Library, ME

Mary

Mary
Funny and artistic
Sibling of Eileen
Lover of dogs and baseball
Who fears clowns and spiders
Who would like to see pigs fly and whales
Resident of Rockledge, PA
Burner
Mary Burner, Grade 3
McKinley Elementary School, PA

Sisters

Sisters are nice
And kinds and sweet, too.
Sisters are
Nice to you —
even when you are mean
to them!
Sisters are smart
And funny, too.
Trinity Duran, Grade 3
Clover Street School, CT

Money

M oney is so nice to have
O n payday, I will go shopping
N o bills to pay today
E xtra money in the bank
Y ou should not waste money
Jaquant Gordon-Jones, Grade 3
Bensley Elementary School, VA

Fall

Fall is as fun as a ball.
You can rake up leaves
And jump in the pile.
Green, yellow, purple, and brown.
Fall, fall, fall, fall.
They all fall down.
In fall it gets colder
Than summer, spring.
Elliott Preble, Grade 2
Eagle's View Academy, FL

My Pumpkin Baby

My pumpkin is a baby,
And she likes to eat all day!
After I feed her,
She always wants to play.
She has four teeth and likes to smile.
She likes to cuddle for just awhile.
If you don't give her what she wants,
She will cry!!!
Bryanna James, Grade 3
Coral Springs Elementary School, FL

The Coolest Angel

My angel is cool.
She does not have to be at school.
She always has a lot of stuff.
Her wings are filled with white fluff.
She likes the pool.
And playing cool!
After much playing,
She begins praying!
Elyssa Chevalier, Grade 3
Coral Springs Elementary School, FL

Uncle

Uncle
Kind, funny
Loving, helping, caring
Strong, careful, tall, skinny
Tio
Ehunixe Lopez, Grade 3
Marie Curie Institute, NY

Dance
Hip Hop, Jazz, Ballet
and Tap too!
They're all different ways
to get up and dance.
Music, fun,
and pretty costumes too!
Welcome to the dance!
Come on, give it a try.
It's easy, it's peasy
if you give it a try!
And it's fun fun fun too!
Sydney Brown, Grade 3
Thoreau Elementary School, MA

Can Camels Catch Crows?
Can camels catch crows?
I've seen a cat catch a mouse.
I've heard a rumor
About a lion eating a tiger.
But can camels catch crows?
I love frogs eating insects.
I hate when bears eat possum.
I've talked about
A shark eating a fish.
But never once have I ever seen
A camel catch a crow.
Justin D., Grade 3
Memorial School, NH

Fall
Red and brown
They all fall down.
My bed is red
Because I like it to match the season.
In fall
I usually have a ball.
I jump in the leaves
With the breeze
Blowing my hair back.
Fall is as fun
As eating a bun.
Amanda Valenzuela, Grade 2
Eagle's View Academy, FL

Apple
A pples are scrumptious when you
P ick them in an apple orchard.
P eel them to make delicious apple pie.
L ittle crunchy apples are so yummy!
E veryone should pick them.
Sara Azzi, Grade 2
Consolidated School, CT

Soccer
Soccer is fun.
I love to run
and to play in the sun.
When I score,
My mom gives a roar!
Amanda Drobnak, Grade 2
Christ the King School, NY

Soccer Soccer Soccer
Soccer is fun with my friends.
I want to kick the ball.
I want to win the game.
I want to learn all the rules.
Then, I will be a soccer kid.
George Romero, Grade 1
Windsor Learning Academy, FL

Shower
Shower
Outside, playground
Slipping, soaking, playing
Showers make you slip
Rain
Crystal Inesti, Grade 3
Marie Curie Institute, NY

Buffalo
Buffalo
City, big
Amazing, exciting, visiting
We visit Niagara Falls
Large City
Philip Hans, Grade 3
Marie Curie Institute, NY

High Merit Poems – Grades K, 1, 2, and 3

Basketball
Basketball
rubber sweat
bumpy hard round
bumps lines brown black
bounces throws passes shoots scores
Karen Troche, Grade 2
Marie Curie Institute, NY

A Day at the Zoo
I had a great time at the zoo.
I saw a turtle, and a zebra,
and a kangaroo.
I rode a pony and saw a monkey, too.
I had a great time at the zoo!
Daniel Sanchez, Grade 1
Mother Seton Inter Parochial School, NJ

Rabbits
Rabbits
stinky dirty
furry warm soft
whiskers eyes ears nose
jumps runs sits smells sees
Ryan Hutchins, Grade 2
Marie Curie Institute, NY

Cats
Cats
dirty smelly
soft furry cute
eyes paws whiskers nose
meow drink eat play sleep
Alize Salcedo, Grade 2
Marie Curie Institute, NY

Christmas
I like Christmas a lot and I believe
in Santa Claus, I believe Jesus was
born on December 25th, and I believe
in Christmas magic.
Dominick Modzelewski, Grade 3
Our Lady of Hope School, NY

Halloween Night
Halloween you get some fright.
With a dark and stormy night.
Pumpkins were lit a little bit.
Called Halloween night.

The ghosts are the host.
To show you gloom and doom.
That scare you to the moon.
Which is a fun night!

Boys are ghosts to scare you the most.
Girls are dolls, prettiest of all.
They were hoping for a toy.
But got a lot of candy O boy!

Now it's time to go to bed.
Our sweet tooth has been fed.
After all, we all fall.
As we curl up like a ball.
Taylor McKay, Grade 3
St Alexis School, PA

Halloween Night
One dark spooky night.
Skeletons came in a flight.
Witches attack on their brooms.
Mummies rise up out of tombs.
The wolves run through the hills.
A vampire sends me chills.
The black cat cried through the dark.
The moon glowed like a spark.
Bats fly to the moon through the trees.
Cats run with scarecrows with honey bees.
We played with the friendly ghost.
And then they ate eggs and toast.
The goblin's howling did scare everyone.
While the skeletons chases us just for fun.
Where the monsters are all seen.
Some are blue, black and even green.
Thomas Szymanski, Grade 3
St Alexis School, PA

A Fall Day

I raked the leaves.
I stuffed them in bags.
Some were stuck in my sleeves.
My dog's tail wags.

The piles were high
And they numbered many.
Some were up to my thigh
Yet somehow, I found a penny.

The day was short
And I was thirsty.
I wanted to play in the fort
But I hurt my knee.

My mom would not let me play.
She said there was too much blood.
I thought I would need an x-ray
Until she said it was just mud!

Ethan Wrobel, Grade 3
St Alexis School, PA

Werewolf

When light fills the moon,
Werewolf's strike.
Claws pop out sharp and pointy,
then faded brown hair pockets out.
White sharp pointy teeth arrive.
Narrow hairy hands.
Werewolves dash and dart.
Near my chamber door,
there's going to be a scary sight.
Its hairy feet clomp around,
and finally it arrives in my room.
I start a loud scream.
He comes closer and closer.
My soul begins to grow stronger.
Lips of black spread apart
then...
his narrow hairy hands come to grab me
But
he can't.
He's my dad.

Danielle Corrado, Grade 3
Oak Ridge Elementary School, PA

Sentence of Doom

I tiptoe in a cave as
silent as a cat.
The earth rumbled.
I found a note.
It was black and gray.
The words were blurry.
I read a sentence.
I read.
Sentence of doom.
Read if you dare to.
What is going on?
This is weird.
A breeze.
Another breezzzzzze.
That was not meeeeeee.
I leave.
I ran as fast as I could,
and got home safe.

Amanda Kroll, Grade 3
Oak Ridge Elementary School, PA

Montessori School

M agical
O utstanding
N urturing
T errific
E nchanting
S uper
S uccessful
O riginal
R eliable
I mpressive

S ociable
C ool
H istorical
O ngoing
O rdinary
L ikable

Harsh Bagdy, Grade 3
Montessori Preparatory School, FL

High Merit Poems – Grades K, 1, 2, and 3

Autumn
A pples are good and sour
U nveil the turkey at the table
T urkey is good with gravy
U se your umbrella for fall rain
M y mom cooks good stuffing and corn
N ear Halloween comes Thanksgiving!
Barbara Saravia, Grade 3
Central Park Elementary School, FL

Autumn
A pples are so sweet to eat
U nder the tree are leaves
T urkey is wonderful
U se pumpkin in your pumpkin bread
M ashed potatoes are very soft
N ever eat green beans on Thanksgiving
Preston Cohen, Grade 3
Central Park Elementary School, FL

Autumn
A pples are good with caramel
U mbrellas are good for raining leaves
T urkey is better with pumpkin pie
U se gravy on turkey and potatoes
M aybe I can have cake and pie
N ooooo! I ate too much!
Sammy Haghnejad, Grade 3
Central Park Elementary School, FL

Autumn
A ll the leaves are falling
U mbrellas are used for rain
T urkey is being eaten
U seful tools are used for cooking
M oms are cooking for feasts
N ative Americans are remembered
Jessica Kaelin, Grade 3
Central Park Elementary School, FL

When Is Thanksgiving?
When helpful Wampanoag hunt
When cozy autumn winds blow
When fresh apple pie bakes
When crazy families have fun
Then it's Thanksgiving.
  Grazie!
Nicolette Moleski, Grade 3
Triangle Elementary School, NJ

Autumn
A pples are a favorite fruit
U p in the tree, where leaves are red
T urkey is my favorite food
U se a lot of spices to make my turkey
M y mom makes great food in autumn
N obody will eat my turkey then.
Rayyan Malik, Grade 3
Central Park Elementary School, FL

What I See
B alls and boats
L akes and lollipops
U niforms
E ggs from robins.
Blake Cubarrubia, Grade 2
Sweetwater Episcopal Academy, FL

Snow
S o cold outside.
N o more sunny days.
O n cold days we have snowball fights.
W ow it is freezing.
Cameron Mitchell, Grade 3
Northeast Elementary School, NY

Dog
Dogs are pets.
Once, my dog broke her leg.
Good dogs get treats.
Anna Bartlo, Grade 1
St Stephen's School, NY

Sun
Shining in the sky
Ball of super heated gas
Gives planet Earth light
Jaslyn Cyr, Grade 2
Weston Elementary School, NJ

What I Found Under My Bed*
A piece of cocoa bubble gum,
A broken red marshmallow gun,
A pencil with a half chewed tip,
A dead frog with a swollen lip,
A glass of milk from a midnight snack,
A broken, rusty, old clothes rack,
Tennis shoes from when I was five,
My pet fish Fred who must have died,
A picture of my grandpa Lou,
A half-filled can of Mountain Dew,
And one more thing, I must confess,
A note from Dad: "Clean up this mess!"

Georgia Bond, Grade 2
Blessed Sacrament School, FL
Patterned after "What I Found in My Desk" by Bruce Lansky

What I Found Under My Bed*
A big red snake,
A dirty rake,
A big green frog,
A rotten log,
A birthday hat,
A little bat,
A broken clock,
A crystal rock,
A paper bag,
A dusty rag,
And one more thing I must confess,
A note from Santa: "Clean up this mess!"

Frankie Storti, Grade 2
Blessed Sacrament Catholic School, FL
Patterned after "What I Found in My Desk" by Bruce Lansky

Long Island Deli
When I'm in the mood for breakfast sandwiches,
I'll be walking to the deli,
To hear the oil crackle in the frying pan,
To watch the cooks stir and splash hot chocolate,
While I stand in line and wait,
I'll be back on occasion,
When I'm in the mood for breakfast sandwiches.

Jake Fiet, Grade 3
Marie Curie Institute, NY

Yummy Chocolate!

I come from...
I look like dark brown, light brown and white
In a warm hand I feel like I am melting
I taste like creamy sugar
I sound crunchy when you bit me
I am the smell of sweetness
I am tasty chocolate!

Brianna Maddonni, Grade 1
Interboro GATE Program, PA

Penguin

P arent penguins take care of their chick until it grows up
E ggs won't hatch until they are ready
N o penguin parent would leave at the same time for food
G ray down covers the baby chick for warmth
U se their flippers to swim
I n the months the mom is gone, the father protects the egg
N ow in five years the young penguin will find a mate

Amanda Giannopoulos, Grade 3
McKinley Elementary School, PA

Penguin

P enguins slide on their bellies
E ggs won't roll away if the dad penguin protects it
N ovember is the month when the chick turns into a junior penguin
G ray is the color of a penguin
U se their beaks to eat fish
I f the daddy penguin protects the egg it won't break
N ear 5 years the penguin is an adult

Owen Bradley, Grade 3
McKinley Elementary School, PA

Fairies

Fairies fly everywhere
Down to earth
Here and there.
High and low
To and fro
With their friends
Off they go.

Emerson DelMonico, Grade 2
Worthington Hooker School – K-2 Campus, CT

Friends

F riends are cool
R eal friends count on each other
I love my friends
E livra is my best friend
N ice friends help you when you need it
D o you love your best friend?
S pecial friendships last forever
Laura Martinez, Grade 3
Bensley Elementary School, VA

4 Little Pigs!

4 little pigs by the light of the sun,
All of them eating cinnamon buns.
The first one says "yum,"
The second one says "yuck."
The third one was licking his chops,
Because the fourth one ate the whole box!
Toby Javage, Grade 3
Shady Grove Elementary School, PA

Fish

I catch fish.
We all like to catch fish.
Fish live in water.
Red fish, blue fish, green fish.
Fish eat worms.
Pink worms, purple worms, black worms.
Brett Moses, Grade 2
Sweetwater Episcopal Academy, FL

When Is Thanksgiving?

When jumbo turkeys roast
When a big table is full
When a cozy family talks
When steaming cider bubbles
Then it's Thanksgiving!
Danke!
Marissa Creelman, Grade 3
Triangle Elementary School, NJ

The Reindeer Party

Dasher gets the chips.
Comet gets the reindeer games.
Rudolph gets the decorations.
Every reindeer goes to the reindeer party.
Ralph Barbieri, Grade 3
Our Lady of Hope School, NY

Snow

S o cold in the winter
N ever really hot in the winter
O n winter days it's fun to run
W e play in the snow
Wilfredo Martinez, Grade 3
Northeast Elementary School, NY

Pups

P layful
U p they jump
P rotect you
S weet and cuddly
Shanelle Herrera, Grade 2
Marie Curie Institute, NY

Deer

D rink from the stream
E ating from the ground
E yes are keen
R unning around
CJ Durinick, Grade 2
Marie Curie Institute, NY

Fantasy

I see a statue, and I smile at him.
He smiles back at me.
We talk to each other.
What a complete FANTASY.
Christine Ruggiero, Grade 2
Sweetwater Episcopal Academy, FL

High Merit Poems – Grades K, 1, 2, and 3

Christmas

The snow is twinkling in the sun
like a diamond having fun!
The way I sleep on Christmas day,
is like a kitten tired from play.
Curled up on the couch by noon,
like a cat on a rug...dreaming soon.
I wake up and get my parents to open presents on a Church day.
I play in the snow...like
leaving footprints to and fro...
Poems are fun to read and write indoors
on cozy days as daddy snores...
Merry Christmas to all and of course to you...
and good luck in the year that is new.

Ana Costanzo, Grade 2
St John the Apostle Catholic School, VA

Art

Splitter, spatter all around,
With crayon lines all over the table,
Wishing you will use them first,
You'll use orange, red, no yellow, of course!

Paint splatters all over the room,
Here and there,
There's paint splats everywhere!

The table is colorful
On accident, of course,
If you went in there,
You'd be screaming, "What happened?"

Riley Chou, Grade 3
Memorial School, NH

Fall

Beautiful, colorful leaves drifting away and swiftly falling to the ground,
Sweet apple pie smells floating through the crisp, fresh air,
The crunchy leaves crunching under my feet and little squirrels paws crunching the leaves,
Sweet apple pie melting in my mouth and slipping down my throat,
The cool, crisp breeze blowing against my face
And the warmth of my home.

Caleb Quartararo, Grade 2
Wellington School, FL

Skate Park

When I'm in a skating mood,
I'll be skating in the skate park,
To hear the boards hit the ground,
To watch people do cool tricks,
While I skate in the park,
I'll be back again next summer,
When I'm in a skating mood.
Dylan McComsey, Grade 3
Marie Curie Institute, NY

The Zoo

I went to the zoo,
I saw an elephant,
I saw a tiger,
I saw a rabbit,
I saw a zebra, too.
I went to the zoo, next
time I will go with you!
Samuel Maldonado, Grade 1
Mother Seton Inter Parochial School, NJ

Winter

Children playing in snowball fights.
Kids laughing and screaming...
Making snowmen that are so cute.
Helping Dad set up Christmas lights.
Helping Mom set up the tree.
Hot cocoa sitting right at your seat.
Cookies, crunchy and sweet!
Alyssa Nygaard, Grade 2
St John the Apostle Catholic School, VA

The Zoo

I see the snake
I see an elephant
I see a lion
I see a zebra
I see a sea lion
I see many things
at the zoo.
Samuel Merced, Grade 1
Mother Seton Parochial School, NJ

Golden Corral

When I'm in the mood for fried chicken,
I'll be eating at the Golden Corral,
To hear people crunch on their food,
To watch people walk up to the counter,
While I munch on my fried chicken,
I'll be back again next month,
When I'm in the mood for fried chicken.
Kaitlynn Lehr, Grade 3
Marie Curie Institute, NY

My School

My school is fun. I like school
because I play with my friends.
I learn how to read and write.
We learn how to share. My school
is fun and everyone cares. My school
is a fun place to be, it makes me
very happy!
Valentina Chifa, Grade 1
Mother Seton Inter Parochial School, NJ

Thanksgiving

I like turkey
N ovember is awesome
D ads and moms gather the food
I give thanks
A pple pie
N obody miss the feast
S hare the turkey
Nicholas Pira, Grade 2
St Agatha School, NY

Fall

Fall is coming
Time to play with the leaves
My family is yelling
My brother runs
And it's time to eat treats
Look up in the sky
And catch some leaves
Serena Lim, Grade 2
Children's Village, PA

High Merit Poems – Grades K, 1, 2, and 3

When Is Thanksgiving?
When lovable families dance,
When delicious turkeys get sliced,
When golden-brown ham gets carved, and
When ecstatic parades march,
Then it's Thanksgiving!
Salamat po!
Sydney Rizalinda A. Salvacion, Grade 3
Triangle Elementary School, NJ

School
Nurse keeps us healthy.
Computer keeps us learning.
Math keeps us on track.
Language Arts keeps us writing stories.
Science keeps us in space.
School keeps us smart.
Emma Heywood, Grade 2
Weston Elementary School, NJ

When Is Thanksgiving?
When juicy turkeys roast
When jumbo parades march
When delicious carrot sticks get eaten
When fresh ham gets devoured
Then it's Thanksgiving!
Toda!
Leah Harris, Grade 3
Triangle Elementary School, NJ

I Like the Zoo
I went to the zoo
to see the elephant squirt water.
I thought it would be fun
if he would squirt me too.
Then I get to see a monkey.
When the day is over I sleep.
Armando Cassarrubias, Grade 2
Windsor Learning Academy, FL

Turkey
70 turkeys
are wobbling and gobbling
through my yard
and the next day
60 more were in my yard
wobbling and gobbling.
Reese Thompson, Grade 2
Southold Elementary School, NY

School Days
S uper
C ool
H appy
O utside play
O bey
L earning
Addison Vaught, Grade 1
St John Neumann Academy, VA

Snowman in a Cup
Snowman in a cup
Snowman in a cup
With bells, with bells
With a single snowflake
With sparkles in a cup
With sparkles in a cup
Brooke Howard, Grade 2
Southold Elementary School, NY

Bagels
I feel the warmness of
the bagel. I hear the toaster
clicking like a horse galloping. I
smell the fresh toasted warm bagel.
I taste the fresh dough formed into an
awesome bagel.
Natalie Calabrese, Grade 3
William M Meredith School, PA

In My Village

When I'm afraid of the dark at night
My grandaddy's hands hold me tight
When I am sad and feeling gray
My auntie's smile brightens my day
When I am lonely with no one to care
My friend is there with funny stories to share
When I am worried and don't know what to do
My mama's comforting words help see me through
I can call my daddy when I'm in a mess
When I need to talk
My teacher is the best
My brother is the one
When I want to have fun
And when I need someone to care
My sister is always there
Our village is a special place
Made of family, friends and preachers
Neighborhoods, Shopkeepers, and Teachers
The village protects us, shapes us, and shows us the way
Helps us make it through each and every day

Joshua Allen, Grade 3
Bensley Elementary School, VA

Love, Family and Friends

I love my whole family
My mom, dad, brother and sister
I love them because they forgive me when I do something bad,
Like hit someone
They say "please don't fight again"
They also help me with my homework
My mom and dad give all my favorite foods:
Mac & cheese, Chinese food, bacon, egg and
Cheese sandwiches, and 5 egg rolls
I show I love them in many ways,
Being nice, respectful, calm
I respect them when they say "behave."
When they say not to do bad things, don't steal money, food or candy
I show them love by kissing, hugging and saying "thank you."
I am happy they are in my life because they are what I need the most
They do funny moves like the Jack-O-Lantern and crafty moonwalk and
The walkie-talkie.

Ansel Muschette, Grade 3
New York Institute for Special Education, NY

High Merit Poems – Grades K, 1, 2, and 3

The Magical Kids

The Magical Kids are the best,
No one compares
We beat the rest.
The teacher we have is out of this world.
She teaches us things from all around the world.
She makes us laugh and makes us smile,
She teaches us things that
We will need.
For that we know we will succeed
Thank you my teacher you are the best
The Magical Kids will beat the rest.

Sebastian Mularczyk, Grade 3
Public School 131, NY

Halloween, Halloween

One Halloween I went trick-or-treating at night.
When I came across a haunted house it gave me quite a fright!
I looked at all the houses; it was really freaky
When I went inside I found its floors were creaky!
I saw a monster with ten eyes
In the deserted kitchen I saw a thing that flies!
In the bedroom I saw a skeleton chanting, "Halloween, Halloween,
We're not afraid to make a scene!"
So I ran home as fast as I could
And when I got home I said, "I hope I have good dreams!"
I knew I would!

Zoe Henry, Grade 2
Wellington School, FL

Christmas is Cool!

I like
Christmas a lot,
because it's not hot.
We don't lay in the sun,
because that's not fun.
I like to play in the snow,
when the wind doesn't blow.
When I get out of bed,
I like to sled.
Christmas is the best Holiday,
no matter what the Easter Bunny has to say!

Clayton Brown, Grade 3
Ellicott Road Elementary School, NY

Climbing a Tree

I start to go
UP, UP, UP.
My neck bends backwards.
I see deep green like algae on a pond.

I hear nature sing around me.
Sunlight fills my soul.
Birds flash color like a rainbow.
They dash and dart.
Squirrels go wild, and the bird is closer.
I hear the crickets sing their pretty song.

The wind sprints up the tree, and I try to catch up.
My sweaty hands lose grip of the tree.
I feel like I'm falling to the bottom of the world.
I feel my legs dangle as if I was hanging from a cliff.
DOWN, DOWN, DOWN.

BOOM! I hit the ground.
My eyes slowly open.
I see stars around my head.
I am going to try again.

Meagan Ball, Grade 3
Oak Ridge Elementary School, PA

Friends

Friendship is a magic tie between you and me
Oh my, oh my...you are always beside me
You are my best friend forever.

I don't care if you're black or white you will always be my
Best friend forever.
We can talk, smile, and even cry.
We can keep each other company and share great secrets.
We can be there for each other and help one another.

Can friendship last a whole lifetime? Yes, it can.
But you need to be there for happy and sad times.
You must always respect each other's differences.
You must always guide each other.
A good friend is the best thing in the whole wide world.

Victoria Kapusi, Grade 3
Public School 131, NY

High Merit Poems – Grades K, 1, 2, and 3

When I Dance…
When I dance I feel like a real dancer.
I glide across the room feeling so graceful.
Dancing across the room I feel so much like a real dancer!
I am connected to dance. I twirl, I whirl, I leap
across the room. When I dance I feel so much
like a real dancer.
Ballet, tap, jazz are all dances that I learn.
No matter what the dance is, it all makes me happy.

Catherine Shewchuk, Grade 1
St John Neumann Academy, VA

Football
F is for Fun, when you go run.
O is for Oakland City, where the Raiders call home.
O is for Oh! Here comes the ball.
T is for Tre' caught the ball.
B is for Ball that needs to get into the Goal.
A is for Awesome Tre' wins the game.
L is for Laughs and fun that's what we want.
L is for Lights from the fireworks.

Tre' Clark, Grade 1
St John Neumann Academy, VA

Me
David
Funny, athletic
Son of Theresa and Pat Profit
Lover of donuts and candy
Who hopes to be a pro football player
Who would like to play for the Indianapolis Colts
Resident of Pennsylvania
Profit

David Profit, Grade 3
McKinley Elementary School, PA

When Is Thanksgiving?
When brown footballs are played
When brave Pilgrims and Native Americans are remembered
When traveling Pilgrims arrived
When happy Pilgrims and Native Americans had a big feast
Then it's Thanksgiving!

Franklin Wasserman, Grade 3
Triangle Elementary School, NJ

Fall Is Here!
I see branches moving
I hear leaves
I smell flowers
I feel wind
I taste pumpkin pie and apple pie
Marissa Ovack, Grade 1
McKinley Elementary School, PA

Leaves/Autumn
Leaves
Red, orange
Changing, falling, crunching
The leaves are falling.
Autumn
Rachael Buhl, Grade 3
Kane Area Elementary/Middle School, PA

Fall Is Here!
I see ghosts
I hear hissing vampires
I smell apples
I feel warm pie
I taste candy
Michael Reed, Grade 1
McKinley Elementary School, PA

Monsters/Mummy
Monsters
Big, mean
Scaring, creeping, chasing
Monsters are so scary!
Mummy
Abigail Langille, Grade 3
Kane Area Elementary/Middle School, PA

I Am a Dreamer
I am a dreamer,
often outside the lines.
My walk is slow,
as I gaze at my surroundings.
Dreamer am I.
Aeven O'Donnell, Grade 3
Buckley Country Day School, NY

Love
Love in the sky
We met and said good-bye.
It went bye bye
My face asked why?
What is on your mind?
Are you really blind
He said the sun is in my eyes
It makes me cry
I started to think
This funny love isn't for me
The night rolls in
How odd his eyes
Closed again, I asked why
The night time is mine
I noticed his skin so pale
He looks at me with a long stare
I realized this funny love
Would only be at night
So I'm saying no
So I won't live in fright
Angela Dell, Grade 3
Windsor Learning Academy, FL

Birthdays
Birthdays come but once a year,
I hold that day very dear.

People have them here and there,
With parties going on everywhere.

Birthdays are nice as can be,
Everyone has one you see.

Boys, girls, and families too,
They celebrate them with me and you.

A day of happiness all around,
With lots of presents to be found.

So let's enjoy another year,
And face your age without fear.
Desmond Spady, Grade 3
Windsor Learning Academy, FL

High Merit Poems – Grades K, 1, 2, and 3

Little Bird

Little bird in the tree, yes, yes you come down to me.
So we can play all night and day, oh, oh please stay.
Please little bird, don't go anywhere!
Maybe you can come to my home and have some food.
But please, oh please don't be rude.
My parents and brothers are all scared of birds.
So that makes them all into nerds.
If you fly away, I won't care. I can see you anywhere.
So the bird flew off; far, far away.
Soon we will meet each other again someday.

Deanna Campbell, Grade 3
Blue Lake Elementary School, FL

Autumn Thrills

As the sun sets with heavy eyes,
It displays a good evening show,
With a splash of Pink, Orange and Yellow.
Turning the beautiful bright green into a Yellow, Orange, Gold and Red trees,
The leaves fall sleepily on our land and sleep with the sun.
A beautiful canvas layers our country with colors of Oranges, Chocolate,
Pomegranate and Lemons.
Autumn has arrived!
These colors of trees and our canvas is...
An Autumn Thrill.

Kavya Borra, Grade 3
Dutch Neck Elementary School, NJ

My Apple Tree

Apple tree, oh deciduous tree,
How do you grow, I wonder please?
With oval leaves of inches three,
I bet you grow no taller than me.
But when we met that sunny day,
Oh my, oh my, you took my breath away.
You were taller than I could think,
Great big branches and white flowers
With a hint of pink.
Oh apple tree, oh apple tree.

Korey Aberdeen, Grade 2
Public School 235 Janice Marie Knight, NY

Winter Rocks

C ool presents under the tree
H aving family parties
R acing children running down the stairs
I ce falling down from the sky
S anta Claus is coming to town
T errific presents under my tree
M aking hot chocolate with marshmallows
A nd wonderful cookies and milk
S now falling all around

Guido Modano, Grade 3
Our Lady of Hope School, NY

My Life as a Pilgrim

My life was very interesting
I never knew what was going to happen next
A storm or something
And we had to fish for our food
It was hard to make clothes for people
But we had some fun along the way
At night we would sit by the fire and tell stories
I love to go on voyages because I like to discover new things
And that was how I lived.

Claire O'Shaughnessy, Grade 3
St Mary School, NY

When Is Thanksgiving?

When steaming turkeys roast
When sweaty football players run
When my extended family drives to my house
When colorful leaves fall
Then it's Thanksgiving!
    Danke!

Gabriella Pertab, Grade 3
Triangle Elementary School, NJ

Kids/Innocence

Kids
Youthful creatures
Running, skipping, playing
Rockets filled with fuel
Innocence

Levi Ariker, Grade 2
Worthington Hooker School – K-2 Campus, CT

High Merit Poems – Grades K, 1, 2, and 3

The Sea of Sleep
The sea of sleep
Slowly quietly peacefully sways
Sharks swim by faraway islands
Whisper to the seals and snakes
The sound a sweet new song
Swaying talking otters chattering to each other
The sea of sleep
Gentle jewels are like the sharks fierce eyes
Drifting floating streaming colors
From the sea foam in the waves
Over many and many a million years

Allie Rumberger, Grade 3
Jeffrey Elementary School, CT

Promote Peace
We need to care about each other, not doing any harm.
Working, loving, caring, remaining in God's charm.

Be nice, don't fight, respect one another.
For God created you and your brother.

Share ideas and help each other.
Always be kind to your mother.

If we do that in all our families,
Then it can snowball to all other countries.

Sarah McCombe, Grade 2
Our Lady of Mercy Regional School, NY

Connor
Connor
Brown haired, tall, cool, nice
Son of Kerry and Mike
Brother of Sarah
Hockey, sports, candy
Who likes baseball, football, cupcakes
Who hates squash, Mario Kart
Who would like to rich, be a famous football and baseball player
Resident of Grand Island
Berlinger

Connor Berlinger, Grade 2
St Stephen's School, NY

My Little Pine Tree
There is a little pine tree
Right in the neighbor's yard
And every time I touch it
It pricks me very hard
I don't like the pine tree
Because it pricks me all the time.

Brandon Knights, Grade 2
Public School 235 Janice Marie Knight, NY

Why I Love Pets
I love pets because they are cute,
And sometimes they like to chew on my boot,
There are many types of pets,
And fishermen get the big fish from nets,
There are dogs, cats, birds and fish,
And in their heads, they might have a wish.

Elizabeth Moschello, Grade 3
St James School, NJ

I Love Winter
Winter is my favorite seasons
all the plants go and die
but I hope to say goodbye,
then the bell goes ding,
even when we get to stay home from school,
outside is very cool.

Abigail Stripeikis, Grade 3
St Mary's School, NJ

Snow Falling
The snow is falling
Children can't wait to play in the snow.
Children laughing, people passing.
People saying these days are the best of all.

Christopher Flood, Grade 3
Our Lady of Hope School, NY

Water
Splash the water goes
The waves make a lot of noise
But the fish don't care

Joseph Guenoun, Grade 2
Virginia A Boone Highland Oaks Elementary School, FL

High Merit Poems – Grades K, 1, 2, and 3

Crazy Dogs
My dogs are cute, my dogs are small,
Danyko likes to eat a rock and a ball,
Spike is funny with his mighty bark,
He is scared of the dark,
I love them so much and they love me
Danyko likes to bark at leaves on the tree,
In the winter they jump in the snow,
When they bark my family and I say "NO."

John Cagnassola, Grade 3
St James School, NJ

School
In school my teacher's name is Miss Lisset,
She's been nice to me since the first day we met.

She likes to look at my work when I get done,
She gets happy with me then we have some fun.

Third grade isn't easy at all,
But Miss Lisset won't let me fall!

Alejandra Perez, Grade 3
Windsor Learning Academy, FL

Can You?
Can you hum like a whale?
Can you float like a trout?
Can you hunt like a shark?
Can you swim like a dogfish?
Can you camouflage like a flounder?
Can you jump like a salmon?
Can you carry babies in a pouch like a sea horse?
Can you?

Dominic Rozance, Grade 1
Blessed Sacrament School, FL

Christmas Cookies
Gingerbread cookies are yummy and tasty.
I love how they smell so cinnamony and spicy.
Fragile, crispy gingerbread cookies taste sweet, delicious and scrumptious
When I take a bite I hear, "Crunch!"
I love gingerbread cookies.

Katie Katella, Grade 3
Riverton Public School, NJ

A Celebration of Poets – East Grades K-3 Fall 2010

Santa Is Coming
Santa is Coming!
I have a very big smile!!
I am so glad because he is
coming in a little while.
The cookies are done.
The stockings are hung!
It's time to give a cheer
because Christmas is here!!
Alexis Geras, Grade 3
Our Lady of Hope School, NY

Snowmen
Snowmen are cold
Snowmen melt
Snowmen are snowflakes
I love snowmen
With a carrot nose
Buttons, sticks
And snow, I still love snowmen
Snow is a sign of snowmen
Jullianna Conway, Grade 2
Southold Elementary School, NY

Football
F ace mask
O ffense
O vertime
T ouchdown
B reak
A wesome
L aces
L unge
Zack Brown, Grade 3
Walnut Street Elementary School, NJ

Me
Ezra
Smart, strong
Sibling of Jacob and Sophie
Lover of pets and ice cream
Who hopes to have a dog
Who would like to be an inventor
Resident of Jenkintown
Taylor
Ezra Taylor, Grade 3
McKinley Elementary School, PA

Football
F ast
O utstanding
O rdinary
T all
B all
A wareness
L earn
L ong
Ryan Phillips, Grade 3
McKinley Elementary School, PA

Snack
My favorite snack is Oreos
I wish I had some more.

They make me feel real good
In my tummy oh so yummy!

Man I love my Oreos
From my head to my toes.
Tyler Sisson, Grade 3
Bensley Elementary School, VA

Bella
Bella is a baby.
Excellent, good, Bella.
Little Bella is still good.
Lots of people love Bella.
A dog loves Bella.
Isabella Kelley, Grade 1
St Stephen's School, NY

Winter
Winter is snowy
Snowball fight with my brother
Shivering cold
Sipping hot cocoa
Warming by the fire
Gianna Gesimondo, Grade 2
St Mary's School, NJ

My Favorite Dad

I love my grandfather.
I call him "Dad."
He's like a dad to me.
He treats me well.
He comes to my basketball games.
He takes me to Playland and
I live with him.

He's funny.
He does interesting and fun games on the PS2
Like *Snoopy versus the Red Baron*
And *Ace Combat IV* and *V*.
Sometimes in the morning, we wrestle each other.
He laughs. I laugh. We
both laugh.

It's a good thing he's in my life.
If it weren't for him, who'd…?
Well, I just love my grandfather
He's my favorite dad.

Nicholas Chimelis, Grade 3
New York Institute for Special Education, NY

I Forgive My Princess

I forgive my little Chihuahua, Princess
For chewing my little shoes.
I get a little angry,
But I don't want to hit my dog!
Because I love her.

When I forgive her, I give her a chew toy
And a bubble bath.
She loves when I blow bubbles for her.
I love my Princess and I forgive her now

Because when I first met Princess, she did not know me,
But when I put my hand up to her she sniffed it
And now she knows me and
I like that.
I forgive my Princess.

Myeeka Jones, Grade 2
New York Institute for Special Education, NY

A Celebration of Poets – East Grades K-3 Fall 2010

One Halloween Night
One Halloween night
Became a fright
Three ghosts appeared
Each wearing a white beard

Then came a bat
That flew off with my hat
My candy I kept tight
When a vampire asked for a bite

A werewolf did howl
Which made me scowl
I ran for cover
When some mummies came over

I ran from Frankenstein
Who had lost his mind
I ran past a gnome
To get to my home

It was so dandy
To finally eat my candy
Matthew Miller, Grade 3
St Alexis Catholic School, PA

How to Fly a Poem
Write a poem
Tie it to a string
Fling it in the air
Watch it zang-zing
Watch it fly
Puncturing the air
Watch it not tear
Papery and leathery
Sharp as a knife
Watch it sail
Through the night
Fiery feathery
Bright as a ball
Watch it, watch it,
Watch it not fall.
Alexander Allison, Grade 3
Thoreau Elementary School, MA

Halloween Night
Jack-O-Lanterns glowing in the night,
I prepared myself for a fright.
With a pillowcase over a shoulder,
I thought that I better get bolder.

On my way out the door,
I almost fell to the floor.
Standing there in front of me,
Was a kid dressed like a huge bumblebee!

Mom reminded me to be polite,
And do not go beyond her sight.
She said that I may say trick-or treat,
But never should I smell my feet.

After walking so many blocks,
I wore holes in my dirty socks.
Halloween Eve was really dandy,
Now I get to eat my candy.
Camille Cunningham, Grade 3
St Alexis School, PA

The Beautiful Day
Birds flying and leaves drifting
on the ground fast.
Fruits appear on trees.
Birds sing on top of the trees.
I try to give them seeds,
but they fly away.
The leaves are still alive.
A golden sun
up in the sky
looks like a golden rose looking at me.
A garden path
that leads to the golden flowers
blooming in my garden.
Bees landing on flowers
and getting honey.
Grasshoppers hopping under
my deck.
The greatest day in my garden.
Hurayrah Malik, Grade 3
Oak Ridge Elementary School, PA

Christmas

C hristmas cookies are very yummy
H ere is a gingerbread house
R ush to the stores
I decorate the tree and cannot wait until Christmas day
S anta Claus is coming yelled the children
T he children dance and sing
M erry Christmas everyone
A fun and jolly holiday
S o much fun on Christmas Eve

Julia Cybulka, Grade 3
McKinley Elementary School, PA

Skytrains

S ilent
K ind people working inside
Y ou'll like its windows and seats
T errific rides
R uns on railroad tack high above the ground
A mazing electric powered train
I ncredibly huge stations
N eeds electricity to run
S uper-fast speed

Marwynn Somridhivej, Grade 3
Wapping Elementary School, CT

The Rock Star

My pumpkin is a rock star,
He loves to eat some candy bars.
He loves to play the lead guitar.
He likes to do it under the stars.
He wears make-up as a disguise.
But, I don't think the audience really minds.

Dylan Byerly, Grade 3
Coral Springs Elementary School, FL

Snakes

Snakes
Creepy creatures
Slithering, spying, snacking
Venomous villains
Hunters

Daniel Trastsianka, Grade 2
Worthington Hooker School – K-2 Campus, CT

A Celebration of Poets – East Grades K-3 Fall 2010

How I Promote Peace
I promote peace
by not fighting with
my little brother.
He might cry.
He's much smaller
than me.
I could hurt him.
When he's upset
I try to make him
happy by
dancing and hopping
around.
I make him laugh.
Angelina Bokina, Grade 1
Our Lady of Mercy Regional School, NY

My Family Drive
Once my family drove far.
My dad drove the car.
My sister was napping.
My brother was tapping.
I was snacking.
The car started screeching.
My dad started weeping.
Ugh!
We had a flat tire.
I thought I saw a little fire.
My dad put it out.
My sister started to shout.
IT WAS A MESS!
Kimberly Conmy, Grade 3
Interboro GATE Program, PA

High Rollers
When I'm in the mood to skate,
I'll be skating at High Rollers,
To hear the people scream,
To watch the kids skate,
While I skate around,
I'll be back again next weekend,
When I'm in the mood to skate.
Talisha Muniz, Grade 3
Marie Curie Institute, NY

Harry Potter
Harry Potter is the best wizard
I ever knew.

He is very good in class
Which means Voldemort cannot last.

On his broomstick he is very fast
He hardly ever has a crash.

He is very nice to Ron and Hermione
They use magic to fight the enemy.

He always tries to help people out
He is a great hero without a doubt.
Brock Duma, Grade 1
St John Neumann Academy, VA

Fall
In fall I see
The colorful leaves falling
What do *you* see?
I see the kids jumping in leaves
What do *you* see?
I see the leaves falling on the ground
What do *you* see?
I see people raking
What do *you* see?
I see the landscapers cleaning yards
What do *you* see?
I see the leaves changing colors
What do *you* see?
Amani Levitan, Grade 3
Clover Street School, CT

Trees
The trees swing in the breeze
Reminding me of coconut trees
Florida is a good place to go
To see those trees blow and flow
I look up high above my head
I just want to faint upon my bed.
Kelsey O'Sullivan, Grade 3
John Lyman School, CT

High Merit Poems – Grades K, 1, 2, and 3

Candy

C omes with freaky wrappers only in fall.
A wesome candy smells delicious.
N o one can resist the sweet taste.
D ing donging the doorbells.
   Collecting in your bag.
Y ou can't resist the awesome candy
   when you look at it.

Kassidy Collentine, Grade 2
Consolidated School, CT

Penguin

P rotect baby chick is the job of the father
E ats fish
N eeds food to live
G rows up quickly
U nbelievably cold in Antarctica
I n the freezing cold they live
N ever hot

Matthew Gallagher, Grade 3
McKinley Elementary School, PA

Marissa

My friend is Marissa
A friend is someone that you met
Run with me
I like to play with Marissa
Sometimes I play with her
So then we play a game
And we play tag

Samantha Falbo, Grade 1
St Stephen's School, NY

Science

S cientific
C lues and answers
I ncredible
E verything I like
N othing is boring
C an be confusing
E xpert only

Azaria Lewis, Grade 3
Bensley Elementary School, VA

Bad Pumpkin

My bad, bad pumpkin!!
My pumpkin is so bad.
He makes the kids so sad.
His jacket is red.
His dad's name is Ted.
With glasses so blue.
Don't let him near you!!

Matthew Rivera, Grade 3
Coral Springs Elementary School, FL

Shy and Sad Pumpkin

My pumpkin is shy but not very happy.
She is a baseball player,
Who plays for the YANKEES.
She has pretty pink hair,
And her eyes are pink too!
She didn't make a hit,
And that is why she is blue

Karina Rogowski, Grade 3
Coral Springs Elementary School, FL

Love All Around

I'm going to miss you so I kiss you goodbye.
I miss you so I come after you.
When I see you, I hug you.
We walk back home.
I'm not worried,
Now that you're here with me.

Quinton Anderson, Grade 3
Lawnton Elementary School, PA

Exciting Scooter

I come from…
I look like wobbly plastic
I feel the hard driveway
I taste the fall air
I hear kids talking
I hear kids laughing
I am a riding scooter!

Emma Donnelly, Grade 1
Interboro GATE Program, PA

A Celebration of Poets – East Grades K-3 Fall 2010

Thankful
T urkey
H ugs
A frica
N est
K ittens
F ish
U s
L ove
Andrew Brand, Grade 1
St Mary's School, NJ

Thankful
T urkey
H ugs
A pples
N ovember
K ids
F riends
U nited States
L ord
Perrin Limey, Grade 1
St Mary's School, NJ

Thankful
T ap shoes
H ats
A frica
N uts
K itten
F lags fading
U ncles
L ove and lips
Anika Ordas, Grade 1
St Mary's School, NJ

Art Art Art!
To make this school a better place
I would become an art teacher
Drawing, crafts, and macaroni art
Are some things we would do
Art makes me feel like I'm glowing
Joseph Campbell, Grade 3
Fairview Elementary School, PA

Leaf
Little green leaf
With fiery red edges
Patches of orange
On its crinkly skin
Brown stem stand
Tall and straight
Sara Burgos, Grade 2
Carlyle C Ring Elementary School, NY

Winter
W inter is fun.
I ce is falling down.
N o more waiting to jump in the snow.
T o make hot chocolate you need help.
E ager to see Santa Claus.
R eindeer are taking a rest.
Emilio Gallo, Grade 3
Our Lady of Hope School, NY

Skeleton/Skull
Skeleton
Bony, creepy
Hiding, scaring, shaking
Skeletons shake a lot.
Skull
Brennan Smith, Grade 3
Kane Area Elementary/Middle School, PA

Candy/Chocolate
Candy
Yummy, sticky
Looking, tasting, eating
It is all gone!
Chocolate
Ian O'Hara, Grade 3
Kane Area Elementary/Middle School, PA

Winter Fun
Lots of snow outside
Sledding down a hill is great
So much fun to do
Mia Schneider, Grade 2
St Mary's School, NJ

High Merit Poems – Grades K, 1, 2, and 3

Shawn

Shawn
Funny and active
Sibling of Nick McConnell
Lover of Reese's and my dog Chase
Who fears black holes and outer space
Who would like to see Spain and the World Cup
Resident of Huntingdon Valley, PA
McConnell

Shawn McConnell, Grade 3
McKinley Elementary School, PA

Sean

Sean
Funny and friendly
Sibling of Sophia
Lover of video games and food
Who fears bears and sharks
Who would like to see Disney World and outer space
Resident of Rockledge, PA
Lamb

Sean Lamb, Grade 3
McKinley Elementary School, PA

Anthony

Anthony
Athletic and kind
Son of Dawn and Dave
Lover of ice hockey, food
Who fears nothings
Who would like to see Mike Richards and a Flyers game
Resident of Rockledge, PA
Lombard

Anthony Lombard, Grade 3
McKinley Elementary School, PA

Fall

Beautiful, colorful leaves gently falling to the ground,
The smell of pie gracefully floating to my nose,
Leaves crunch under my feet,
Pumpkin pie deliciously melting in my mouth,
Cold leaves falling softly on my hands.

David Stenzel, Grade 2
Wellington School, FL

Me

I'm smart
I'm cute

Funny and sweet too
Love to be myself

I love to play with my friends
It's nice to be me
Danixi

Danixi Perez, Grade 1
Public School 105 Senator Abraham Bernstein, NY

Princess Baby

My pumpkin is a Princess Baby.
I ask her if she likes pie, and she says, "Maybe."
She asks me to collect shells.
She also collects lots of bells.
She has a pretty dress.
But she is never a mess.
She has nice, sweet blue eyes,
And an orange smile.
I don't know why.

Viviana Jimenez, Grade 3
Coral Springs Elementary School, FL

My Pilot Pumpkin

Amelia loves to fly.
Up, up in the nice, blue sky.
And she's a female pilot!
She has goggles when she flies,
And wears red earrings too.
She also has a bright pink scarf and yellow eyes! Not blue.

Nicole Healey, Grade 3
Coral Springs Elementary School, FL

Our Flag

Our flag,
Red, white and blue!
It hangs at our capital
For me and for you!
Our flag!

Steven Zhang, Grade 2
Worthington Hooker School – K-2 Campus, CT

High Merit Poems – Grades K, 1, 2, and 3

Recycle

Recycle the waste
It will help the earth
Make it clean as a house
Pick the trash and put it into the can
Everybody do as much as possible
Then our home of world will become prettier and safer

Abinaya Ravichandren, Grade 3
Abington Avenue Elementary School, NJ

Snow

Winter is fun!
Did you know I like the snow?
I love the sun, but not when it melts the snow!
Snow, snow, snow, I want to know
How do you come and go?
Snow is fun but don't forget to bundle up!

Josephine Ferriso, Grade 3
Our Lady of Hope School, NY

Santa's Gingerbread Man

As I bake the gingerbread man,
The air is filled with a special scent that makes me hungry.
When I take him out and look at him
I know Santa will love him.
When Santa comes he can't wait to eat the gingerbread man.
When he does, I can hear him say, "Yumm!"

Fisher Hudak, Grade 3
Riverton Public School, NJ

Cell

C hloroplast are only in plant cells
E very cell has a brain
L iving things have cells all over them
L ots of cells in a person's body

Taylor Huyck, Grade 3
Susquehanna Community Elementary School, PA

Nature

Water helps trees grow
Waterfalls are wonderful
Bees fly in the air

Karina Lee, Grade 2
Virginia A Boone Highland Oaks Elementary School, FL

Cheer Day

Hooray it's cheer day!
I wake up excited to see my friends and family.
Dressed in my blue, gold, and white,
And making sure everything is just right,
I am smooth and all too cute,
Just look at me while I shoop shoop shoop.
Hooray it's cheer day!
The sky is blue and the sun is out,
So let's hear you shout.
I am happy and all I can say is
Hooray it's cheer day!

Brionna Conyers, Grade 2
Nellie K Parker Elementary School, NJ

My Mom the Princess

I love my mom
My mom is the princess character from
Super Mario brothers
She is like a princess
She plays video games with me
She gets me food
I like it when she orders pizza
I give her hugs to show that I love her
I am happy she is in my life
I laugh when she tells jokes
She is really good at telling jokes

Benjamin Cobarrubia, Grade 3
New York Institute for Special Education, NY

My Sister

My sister is as soft as a teddy bear
Her skin is as smooth as silk
I snuggle with my sister every day
She keeps me warm and cozy
My sister is as cute as a kitten
And as playful as a puppy
I love my sister as much as I love life itself
Hugging her is better than playing with my toys
My sister turns my world into happiness
I have to hug and kiss my sister every day and night
I love you so much my precious baby sister, Melanie Maria.

Vanessa Guadalupe Ramos, Grade 3
Public School 131, NY

Michael

Michael
Funny and athletic
Son of Lindsay and Patrick
Lover of chocolate marshmallows and peanut butter
Who fears scary movies and whales
Who would like to see Ireland and Brazil
Resident of Rockledge, PA
McGinnis

Michael McGinnis, Grade 3
McKinley Elementary School, PA

Joseph

Joseph
Caring and fair
Sibling of Olivia, Morgan, Billy, and Kevin
Lover of pumpkin pie and ice cream
Who fears jumping six stairs on roller blades and pythons
Who would like to see the Bahamas and Abraham Lincoln
Resident of Jenkintown, PA
O'Brien

Joseph O'Brien, Grade 3
McKinley Elementary School, PA

Eli

Eli
Funny and fun
Son of Debra and Bill
Lover of the game *Plants vs Zombies*
Who fears poison ivy and sharks
Who would like to see the Harry Potter Park and the White House
Resident of Rydal, PA
MacDonald

Elias MacDonald, Grade 3
McKinley Elementary School, PA

Burgers

Burgers have cheese
With ketchup, mustard and pickles please, make it extra on the go
And add onions, lettuce and tomatoes you know.
With the meat between each bun
Please give me a soda and fries for fun.

Phillip Lubowiecki, Grade 3
Windsor Learning Academy, FL

Can You?

Can you purr like a cat?
Can you sleep like a dog?
Can you hiss like a snake?
Can you fly like a bird?
Can you run like a fox?
Can you jump like a frog?
Can you crawl like a lady bug?
Can you?

Aaron Hummer, Grade 1
Blessed Sacrament School, FL

Can You?

Can you stand still like a turtle?
Can you soar like a bird?
Can you hiss like a snake?
Can you sneak like a cat?
Can you lie like a clam?
Can you fly like a butterfly?
Can you hop like a frog?
Can you?

Adriana Cortez, Grade 1
Blessed Sacrament School, FL

Me

Livia
Smart, funny
Daughter of David and Beth
Lover of Buddy, Milly, and my family
Who hopes to be famous when she is old
Who would like to be rich
Resident of Pennsylvania
Kleiner

Livia Kleiner, Grade 3
McKinley Elementary School, PA

Cat

Cat
Cute, funny
Eating, drinking, sleeping
They are so small
Kitten

Emilio Nieves, Grade 3
Marie Curie Institute, NY

Can You?

Can you bite like a shark?
Can you run like a cheetah?
Can you bark like a dog?
Can you swim like a fish?
Can you waddle like a penguin?
Can you hunt like a polar bear?
Can you splash like a whale?
Can you?

R.J. Freyesien, Grade 1
Blessed Sacrament School, FL

Baseball

Catch the ball
Pitch the ball
Hit the ball
Run!
It's out of the park!
First
Second and third
Homerun!!!

Harry Bifulco, Grade 2
Southold Elementary School, NY

Fall

Fall is windy.
You see leaves
Floating in the air.
You see red, green, and brown too.
It is fun
To rake the leaves
Into a bed
And jump in it!

Dillon Rowland, Grade 2
Eagle's View Academy, FL

Spider

Spider
Mean, silent
Eating, spinning, walking
Scary, black, crawling, poison
Tarantula

Japhet Valentin, Grade 3
Marie Curie Institute, NY

High Merit Poems – Grades K, 1, 2, and 3

My Two Loves
I love both
My mom and my Aunt April.
They buy me toys, Legos.
They cook delicious food.
They make me happy.
We play outside with the family
We play catch
So I hug and kiss them.
They're my two loves!

Jaylen Gregory, Grade 2
New York Institute for Special Education, NY

Christmas
C ute little toys wrapped around the tree
H appy smiles on everybody's faces
R ace over to your presents
I s it a board game?
S o much fun celebrating this special holiday
T he house is filled with joy
M ust go get hugs from my mom
A wonderful day of happiness
S o much snow on this day

Katherine Reyes, Grade 3
Northeast Elementary School, NY

Super Hero Pumpkin
My super hero pumpkin has a great disguise.
He has a long green mustache,
And bright yellow eyes!
He likes to fight the bad guys.
And wherever he goes,
he always flies!

Malachai Johnpoll, Grade 3
Coral Springs Elementary School, FL

Drawing
…Just a little slip of paper
With some markings on it too
Don't you wonder how it happened?
…Just a bunch of little lines
Make a little me and you

Margo Pedersen, Grade 2
Worthington Hooker School – K-2 Campus, CT

The Moon

The moon rotates around the earth
And goes d
       o
        w
         n

             p.
          p u
       p u
And it goes u

Michael Odzer, Grade 2
Virginia A Boone Highland Oaks Elementary School, FL

Beautiful Pin Oak

As tall as a three story building.
The branches are big and fat.
Small ones are growing out of the big ones.
Some of the branches point up and some across.

The leaves rustle in the wind
They are turning orange, gold, and red.
They have little spikes on the end.
The weather is getting cold.
They finally fall off.

India Phillip, Grade 2
Public School 235 Janice Marie Knight, NY

Big Sister

B eing helpful is a very important part.
I play with them even if it is a baby game.
G ive them lots of love!

S haring my favorite things.
I love my sisters and watch over them.
S ometimes they are annoying.
T hey touch my stuff.
E very day we play together and I teach them things.
R eally I am a lucky girl.

Camden Scout Haynes, Grade 1
St John Neumann Academy, VA

Blue

Blue is the color of the sky.
I look up and wonder why.
A sail boat with a blue sail coming sailing by.
While the other boats coming zooming by.

Cade Armstrong, Grade 2
Sweetwater Episcopal Academy, FL

Winter

Winter is a great season.
The snowman has a tall black hat.
Winter is one of the coldest seasons,
The snowman has a friend named Matt.

Olivia Abeles, Grade 2
Virginia A Boone Highland Oaks Elementary School, FL

Winter

In winter the pool will freeze.
In winter it sometimes snows.
Winter has a cool breeze,
Winter is a cold season.

Robert Behar, Grade 2
Virginia A Boone Highland Oaks Elementary School, FL

Cell

C ells live in your body
E ach cell has a different name
L ittle cells are small
L ots of cells are in your body

Faith Acosta, Grade 3
Susquehanna Community Elementary School, PA

The Magic of Winter

The children are all building snowmen,
My job is to laugh and to play.
I put on my boots and my jacket,
Now I'm ready for a cold winter day!

Nina Horowitz, Grade 2
Virginia A Boone Highland Oaks Elementary School, FL

Sunny Days

Sunny days, sunny skies,
ladybugs and butterflies.
Little bees and big oak trees…
everything is part of spring!

Such sunny days with big bright skies
make this day a paradise!
Oh, sunny days, sunny skies,
ladybugs and butterflies.
Anna Kulikova, Grade 3
Hammond Elementary School, MD

Rainy Night

In my bed I lay
I don't know what to say
Lightning flashes and thunder crashes
In my bed I stay

The rain has a poundy sound
The wind is blowing around
Nothing can I see
Peace is floating around me
Jessica Wang, Grade 3
Maureen M Welch Elementary School, PA

Damon

D amon likes to dance
A n apple is good to eat
M y mom gives me juice to drink
O n Sunday I play in a football game
N ame is Damon
Damon Bradshaw, Grade 3
Bensley Elementary School, VA

Halloween

Haunted houses
bats surrounded
over the roof
ghosts are outside
saying Boo!
If you look!
Mary Lemoine, Grade 1
Dyer Library, ME

Best Friends

B eautiful
E verlasting
S uper fun
T errific

F orever
R espectful
I ncredible
E xciting
N ice
D efending
S pecial
Lindsey Osit, Grade 3
Wapping Elementary School, CT

Fall

Fall is a ball.
There is so much to do.
Who wants to jump in the leaves?
There are so many things to do in the fall.
I want to do them all.
My doorbell rings.
Someone is here.
I wonder if they want to go to the park
That is near.
I hope fall
Is this fun next year.
Ashlynn Auble, Grade 2
Eagle's View Academy, FL

Peace Is…

A waterfall falling down.
Watching TV on a soft couch
Reading a book.
Looking at the sky.
Listening to birds chirping.
Seeing butterflies fly by.
Sleeping on a comfy bed.
Dreaming about calm things.
But most of all,
Peace is relaxing.
Ashley Bond, Grade 3
St Augustine Cathedral School, CT

Natalie
Natalie
Determined and nice
Sibling of Sean
Lover of math and candy
Who fears Lucy and Rita the dogs, and cacti
Who would like to see long division improving and a giant ice cream cone
Resident of Elkins Park, PA
Faye

Natalie Faye, Grade 3
McKinley Elementary School, PA

Emily
Emily
Athletic and caring
Sibling of Liam
Lover of chocolate and sports
Who fears lightning and spiders
Who would like to see pigs fly and Jason Werth
Resident of Rockledge, PA
Friel

Emily Friel, Grade 3
McKinley Elementary School, PA

Alex
Alex
Athletic and funny
Sibling of Avery
Lover of Reese's Peanut Butter Cups and baseball
Who fears Coraline and the dark
Who likes to see the Deathly Hallows movie and Jimmy Rollins
Resident of Elkins Park, PA
Martin

Alexander Martin, Grade 3
McKinley Elementary School, PA

Cookies for Christmas
The gingerbread man smells cinnamony when it comes out of the oven.
When I taste one I say, "Yum!"
The burnt gingerbread man smells like Christmas.
I decorate him with gumdrops and icing.
He waits on a plate for Santa to come.

Thomas Gural, Grade 3
Riverton Public School, NJ

A Celebration of Poets – East Grades K-3 Fall 2010

Gingerbread Man
You are in the oven
but you don't taste like a muffin.
Your icing melts.
You have a licorice belt.
You're fun to make
and easy to bake.
Have fun in my tummy
you are yummy!
Krista DiMaggio, Grade 3
Our Lady of Hope School, NY

Biking
When I go biking, I feel free.
Free like a little bumble bee.
Who will stop me?
Who will get me?
No one.
I will go biking now and forever.
Soon I will rush home and
Jump into my parents' hands.
Olivia Nycz, Grade 3
Sweetwater Episcopal Academy, FL

Thankful
T ogether we are safe.
H ave hot cocoa with marshmallows.
A sk to sit by the fire.
N ever hate someone.
K ids are sleeping.
F un and laughter.
U npack gifts.
L ove and care.
Bibiana Leon, Grade 3
Northeast Elementary School, NY

Football
F ast running back
O pinion on plays
O perations for hurt players
T ouchdown
B leachers
A thletics
L indsey Witten is awesome
L ove it!
William Harper, Grade 3
Wapping Elementary School, CT

Holidays
H anukah
O pening presents on Christmas
L icking Halloween candy
I ce cream on 4th of July
D ays that are fun on Holidays
A merica's Presidents on President's day
Y ucky candy and awesome candy
S ucking chocolate bunnies on Easter
Derek Eppinger, Grade 3
McKinley Elementary School, PA

Me
Grace
Funny and caring
Sibling of Anna
Lover of hamsters and skateboarding
Who hopes to be an artist
Who would like to study art
Resident of Pennsylvania
Kirwin
Grace Kirwin, Grade 3
McKinley Elementary School, PA

Horses
Horses are playmates
They run, jump, and kick
But the best thing is
That you can ride them
Over and over again
Anthony Habeck, Grade 3
St Mary's School, NJ

Alana
A lways respectful
L oves animals
A lways drawing
N ever yelling
A lways eating fruit
Alana Harrison, Grade 3
Bensley Elementary School, VA

High Merit Poems – Grades K, 1, 2, and 3

Peace Is...
A horizon touching the water and the sky.
Relaxing by watching TV.
Playing with my baby brothers.
When I go to Disney World.
A baby sleeping in his bed.
Playing a game.
A song playing.
Reading a book about God.
But most of all,
Peace is in my life.
Isaac DaGraca, Grade 3
St. Augustine Cathedral School, CT

Peace Is...
Calm when I sit by a tree.
Quiet when I'm alone.
Amazing.
Hopeful.
Clouds going away.
Relaxing.
Singing my favorite song.
Going to bed peacefully.
But most of all,
Peace is the sun shining on me.
Benjamin Kirkland, Grade 3
St Augustine Cathedral School, CT

Peace Is...
A sunset.
Like a dove flying.
Mom reading a bed time story.
My baby brother sleeping.
My family together.
A colorful picture.
Like a song.
Relaxing on the couch.
But most of all,
Peace is clouds floating away.
Mbiya Kabongo, Grade 3
St Augustine Cathedral School, CT

Fun Summer Day
Fun day with no rain
Swimming in my pool with friends
Fun days never end
Adrianna Gilgar, Grade 2
St Mary's School, NJ

Cold Winter Day
I love when it snows!
Making angels and snowmen.
My mom likes to play too.
Cameron Uriguen, Grade 2
St. Mary's School, NJ

Vacation
Airplanes, cars, trains
Pool, beach, water slide
Suntan lotion, salt water, fun.
D'Angelo Brice, Grade 2
Weston Elementary School, NJ

A Winter Day
It is snowing now
The snow looks very shiny
I love winter days
Toun Olokungbemi, Grade 2
St Mary's School, NJ

Cold Days
A cold winter day.
Build an enormous snowman.
Drinking hot cocoa.
Brian Pinand, Grade 2
St Mary's School, NJ

Happy Halloween
I love Halloween.
I can't wait till candy time.
My costume is great.
Sydney Sacco, Grade 2
Wanamassa Elementary School, NJ

Thankful

T errific day
H elpful people
A wesome pets
N ever give up
K ids working together
F amilies having a great time
U ndivided attention
L iking each other forever

Avery Martin, Grade 3
McKinley Elementary School, PA

School

I love school,
Every school should have a rule.
I love math it's very fun,
and when I'm in gym we have to run.
Sometimes in art,
we have to take things apart.
When we play ball,
we try not to fall.

Victoria Malec, Grade 3
Ellicott Road Elementary School, NY

Phillies*

I love the fighting Phillies
They are not hillbillies
They hit the ball wham! I am a fan
Phillies are my favorite team
Let's go Phils! you know what I mean.

Go Phillies!

Dylan Maltin, Grade 3
Shady Grove Elementary School, PA
*Dedicated to my cousin

Fall/Autumn

Fall
Windy, colorful
Falling, jumping, screaming
Leaves are falling down.
Autumn

Austin Mitchell, Grade 3
Kane Area Elementary/Middle School, PA

The Trickiest Genie

I once met an evil genie,
who wasn't very nice.
His heart was filled with rotten eggs,
not candy sticks or spice.
I wished for a giant mansion,
instead I got a shed,
filled with mice and skunks
with bald spots on their heads.
I then asked for a limousine
to drive around all day,
but he gave me a bicycle
made out of moldy clay.
I said, "Hey, you tricky genie!
Stop doing this to me!
I wish that I could throw you
as far as I could see."
"The third wish is the one I grant.
You're wish is my command."
So I picked him up and threw him
to a far away land!

Cameron Fillion, Grade 3
Memorial School, NH

How I Promote Peace

When someone is sad,
That makes me feel bad.
Instead of being shy,
I go over and say "Hi."
When someone gets hurt,
Parents hear my alert.

When someone is finding a book,
I help them look.
When there's a sad boy,
I give him a toy.

When someone's alone,
I go over and they hear my happy tone.

When my friend is stuck on a question,
I give them my full attention.

Brynn Madigan, Grade 3
Our Lady of Mercy Regional School, NY

High Merit Poems – Grades K, 1, 2, and 3

Moving
Moving
to
sun
to
moon
from place
to place
from mother
to daughter
from me to you
Sabrina Fierro, Grade 3
William M Meredith School, PA

The Pledge of Allegiance
Like it, like it, like the song
Like it, like it, the pledge
Like it, like it, most of all
Like it, like it, it is fun so far
Is it bad or is it fun?
I think it is fun
I love the pledge most of all
So fun fun fun
So loved loved loved
Kaia Rothman, Grade 2
Southold Elementary School, NY

Love
Love
happiness, peaceful
enjoying, sharing, dating
propose, marry, baby, family
Caring
Maddison Kilmartin, Grade 3
Marie Curie Institute, NY

football
football
tackle, run
guarding, running, kicking
football is my favorite
running back
Brennen Rivas, Grade 3
Marie Curie Institute, NY

Bicycles
Bicycles are fast and furious
They are cool
The wheels are round
With spokes in the surround
They have a seat
Just for one
The handle bars are to hold on
So you can ride with the wind in your face
My bike makes me happy
Nicholas Boccasino, Grade 3
Public School 131, NY

Things at Home
Riding bikes
Playing video games
Watching TV
Drawing pictures
Reading books
Making things with papers
Acting like a super hero
Writing stories
Having fun at home!
Siddhartha Lamsal, Grade 2
Weston Elementary School, NJ

Jack-O-Lantern/Pumpkin
Jack-o-lantern
Orange, round
Smiling, glowing, staring
Watching kids come by
Pumpkin
Athena Strickland, Grade 3
Kane Area Elementary/Middle School, PA

Blocks
Blocks…BLOCKS!!
They are so much fun!
You can build what you want.
Some are square, some are rectangles…
Some are big…some small.
Go and run and build with some blocks.
Mia Adams, Grade 2
St John the Apostle Catholic School, VA

Rabbit/Bunny
Rabbit
Cute, fuzzy
Gathering, scurrying, collecting
Gathering food for winter
Bunny
Madison Lister, Grade 3
Kane Area Elementary/Middle School, PA

Squirrels/Chipmunk
Squirrels
Furry, cute
Running, crawling, hiding
He is very scared.
Chipmunk
Joey Walters, Grade 3
Kane Area Elementary/Middle School, PA

Werewolf/Hombre Lobo
Werewolf
Scary, hairy
Howling, running, sneaking
I'm glad they're fake!
Hombre Lobo
Chad Greville, Grade 3
Kane Area Elementary/Middle School, PA

Ghost
G hosts
H omes they trick or treat in
O dd things happen
S oar in the air on Halloween
T ired of saying "BOO!"
Pisay Meyer, Grade 3
McKinley Elementary School, PA

Witches/Hags
Witches
Green, purple
Haunting, flying, casting
Flying through the air!
Hags
Kortney Good, Grade 3
Kane Area Elementary/Middle School, PA

The Man
There was a man named Sam.
He loved jelly or toast with jam.
He once ate a lot of candy.
So his hair turned really sandy.

The man put the rice in a pot.
In a parking lot.
He knocked on the door.
Then he fell on the floor.
Justin Suber, Grade 3
Bensley Elementary School, VA

Christmas
C heering
H eart
R eally excited
I nside
S now
T ree
M any presents
A nice Christmas story
S itting by the fireplace drinking tea
Emily Ovack, Grade 3
McKinley Elementary School, PA

Shark
S harks will be in the water
H ungry
A ngry
R eally scary
K ills fish
Dillon Brown, Grade 3
Bensley Elementary School, VA

Thanksgiving
F all
A pple pie
M ayflower
I ndians
L et's give thanks
Y ams
Amaya Garcia, Grade 2
St Agatha School, NY

Thanksgiving

T is for turkey.
H is for having friends over
A is for apple pie
N is for no school
K is for knives
F is for full
U is for use left over turkey for turkey sandwiches
L is for loving Thanksgiving because I'm with my family

Avery Tomlinson, Grade 3
Birches Elementary School, NJ

December — My Favorite Month

D ecember is Christmas
E ach Christmas I get a big gift
C hristmas is a holiday
E ach Christmas we get a green Christmas tree
M y dad and mom go shopping
B eing out of school is boring
E ach December is exciting
R omelo is happy on Christmas

Romelo Aleong, Grade 3
Bensley Elementary School, VA

Birthday

B est day of the year!
I s a time to celebrate!
R eady to get older!
T ime of happiness!
H ilarious birthday surprises!
D ay to remember!
A ll your friends come to your birthday party!
Y our day to shine!

Jennette Jacobs, Grade 3
Wapping Elementary School, CT

September

September is when
you play in the sun.
I do go outside
and have a lot of fun.

Melissa Derzavich, Grade 2
Virginia A Boone Highland Oaks Elementary School, FL

Peace Is...

Exciting.
Reading a book.
Watching a bird in a birdbath.
Singing to mom.
Going to the beach.
A family caring for you.
Sleeping like a baby.
Counting the stars at night.
But most of all,
Peace is love.

Jada Lee, Grade 3
St Augustine Cathedral School, CT

Peace Is...

A baby sleeping.
Love for my family.
Exciting.
Sleeping on a soft couch.
Mountains high in the sky.
A sunset of bright orange.
Clouds floating by.
A dove flying away.
But most of all,
Peace is birds chirping in the morning.

Abrien Millington, Grade 3
St Augustine Cathedral School, CT

Ice Hockey

I ce
C heering
E xcellent hockey

H ockey stick
O n the ice
C old ice
K nights
E ven I have fun at hockey
Y eah! We scored!

Logan Crisp, Grade 3
Wapping Elementary School, CT

Peace Is...

Relaxing with mom.
A dove flying.
Praying to the Lord.
Sleeping on my comfy bed.
Going to the Bahamas.
Reading the Holy Bible.
Being with my family.
God healing me.
But most of all,
Peace is being in heaven with God.

Damiane Gaskin II, Grade 3
St Augustine Cathedral School, CT

I Love Thanksgiving

It was Thanksgiving when I woke up,
I was thinking of hot cocoa in a cup.
I love Thanksgiving, that special day,
I would not miss it...there's no way.
I like seeing all the faces
And going to the different places.
I love the turkey that we get.
I play ball with my mitt.
And my sister starts to cry
Because my dad at all the pie.

Isabella Doherty, Grade 3
Helderberg Christian School, NY

Peace Is...

Quiet in the library.
Wonderful.
A stream babbling by.
Clouds floating around me.
A sleeping baby.
Going on a cruise.
Watching a "love" movie.
Relaxing by looking at the mountains.
But most of all,
Peace is a beautiful sunset.

Nathaly Olivo, Grade 3
St Augustine Cathedral School, CT

Halloween Night

On Halloween night I went treating
I could feel my heart beating
I had a lot of fun
I was sad when treating was done

I went back home to get my candy
Who showed up next but Aunt Sandi
She came with bumblebee Alex
Who buzzed, "Give me treats or I'll give tricks"

They came inside for a candy snack
We looked at my lantern named Jack
When they left I was really sad
I closed my eyes and hugged my Dad

I took off my scary makeup
And brought out my Halloween cup
I filled it with candy corn
And slept in bed until the morn'

Kayleigh Robic, Grade 3
St Alexis School, PA

My BFF (Best Friend Forever)

I have a BFF
She is not jealous of anything that I do.
She is caring, understanding, and helpful to me.
She never gives up.
She is always there for me.
Her name is Jiaming Liu
She is my best friend forever!
She is my BFF.

She is pretty just like me.
She is Chinese and different from me.
I know her from second grade.
I am lucky because we are together in third grade.
She is always there to help me and cheer me up.
I love my BFF.

Amena Begum, Grade 3
Public School 131, NY

Halloween Night

My favorite night of the year,
is the night that some may fear.
I will give you many clues,
see if you know what holiday to choose!

On this night, the ghosts come out,
and lots of witches fly about.
Goblins come out and try to scare,
but the Jack-o-Lantern doesn't care.

On this night we get dressed up,
and we get candy and lots of stuff.
We like to go to the Haunted House,
we get real scared and scream at a mouse!

Have I given you enough clues?
Which holiday did you choose?
If you guessed Halloween you're right...
You've won the game...you're out of sight!

Emma Argiro, Grade 3
St Alexis School, PA

Night

Moon lit sky
fills with midnight dreams.
I look toward heaven still.
Moon slides beyond the sky.
Stars whisper.
White pearls shower over me.
It became as dark as outer space,
but with stars shining
just for you to see.
I walk along the dirty street,
as sleepy water drips.
My feet feel like frogs hopping from lily pad to lily pad.
I can hear a soft splash swim into my ear.
The moon shines like blazing hot fire,
but white like a fluffy soft cloud.
A warm dream whispers in my ear...
I hear this...Good night
Good night.

Morgan Kelley, Grade 3
Oak Ridge Elementary School, PA

Trick or Treating

Trick or treating is fun
From house to house we run
We wait until it's dark at night
And I carry my bag and flashlight

Trick or treating is fun
I saw a cowboy with a gun
I saw someone as a bat
And three as a cat

Trick or treating is fun
I never want to be done
I ring the doorbell and say, "Trick or Treat!"
And people give me something sweet

Trick or treating is fun
At the end my bag weighs a ton
At home I dump my candy on the floor
Then I ask my mom, "Can I get some more?"

Daniel Kilburg, Grade 3
St Alexis School, PA

My Stuffed Friends

I have a stuffed lamb and bear.
The bear does not have any hair.
The lamb does not have a tail.
And the bear looks so pale.

They both like to cuddle,
But not in a puddle.

The little, tiny bear is blue.
But the poor lamb has the flu.

The bear is a tiny ant he's so small.
The lamb is like a giant she's so tall.

These are my friends.
Where does this poem end?
I think it ends here.
This friendship poem deserves a big cheer!

Sam Anger, Grade 2
Infant Jesus School, NH

Winter Fun
C ool skates are really great
H aving an awesome time
R acing down hills with sleds
I love winter
S anta Claus is coming down the chimney
T errific time
M aking lots of things
A nd having lots of fun
S now falling from the roof
Ethan Vincent, Grade 3
Our Lady of Hope School, NY

Christmas
C hris
H oliday
R elated
I gloo
S now
T ree
M ichael
A wesome
S anta
Michael Zarwin, Grade 3
McKinley Elementary School, PA

Brains
Brains are so smart
They're an important body part
They think
And they're pink

I go to school
And I'm cool
I am new
And he is too
Enrique Alvarez, Grade 3
Bensley Elementary School, VA

The Date
The date looked so great
But I was so late
He dumped me on a plate
But one thing I got ate

He swallowed feet
But we meet
He was fake
But I got a break
Jordan Campbell, Grade 3
Bensley Elementary School, VA

Rainbows
Rainbows
Colorful, curved
Shining, brightly, blending
Colorful, shiny, awesome, rainbows
Make me smile
Nick Rodecker, Grade 3
Marie Curie Institute, NY

Easter
Easter
Easter eggs
Looking, rushing, finding
Look what is inside
Easter eggs
Francesca DeRosa, Grade 3
Marie Curie Institute, NY

Thanksgiving
T hankful
U eat turkey
R you thankful?
K ids like Thanksgiving
E veryone likes Thanksgiving
Y ams
Angelica Roman, Grade 2
St Agatha School, NY

Thanksgiving
P ies we eat on Thanksgiving
A pple pies we cook
R ead about the Pilgrims
A nd we buy all the food
D rink apple cider
E veryone is eating
Nicholas D'Amore, Grade 3
St Agatha School, NY

Evan

Evan
Helpful and athletic
Sibling of brother Mitchell
Lover of candy and hockey
Who fears bees and cicada killers
Who would like to see explosions and sharks
Resident of Rockledge, PA
Carl

Evan Carl, Grade 3
McKinley Elementary School, PA

Ashya

Ashya
Funny and helpful
Sibling of Makyra, Dajah, and Ava
Lover of cats and wigs
Who fears millipedes and centipedes
Who would like to see Mars and the black hole
Resident of Elkins Park, PA
Storm

Ashya Storm, Grade 3
McKinley Elementary School, PA

Baseball

Big people pitching
Awesome to play
See the ball go through the air
Easy to throw
Balls get thrown
All people cheering
Lots of people
Lots of boos when the other team gets a hit

Davis Shenkman, Grade 3
McKinley Elementary School, PA

Love

Love is the best thing that I know
Listening to music on the radio
Two people sharing something that no one can break
Sharing a picnic by the lake
Love

Ra'Nayah Alston, Grade 3
Number 12 Elementary School, NJ

Halloween

H alloween is when I get a lot of candy
A Halloween party can be very scary
L ine up for the haunted house
L ason was a vampire for Halloween
O ur teacher gave us candy
W e are having so much fun on Halloween
E at candy until your stomach hurts
E ndless night of fun
N ighttime is when I get frightened

Amya Washington, Grade 3
Bensley Elementary School, VA

Friendship

Friendship is what I love and is what I have.
I have a very good friendship with Vanessa Ramos.
I know her since Kindergarten.
We smile and share many things together.
We play and enjoy each other's company.
We are now in the third grade and are there for each other.
Our friendship will grow stronger and stronger.
We will help and guide each other.
That is what friendship is all about.

Savannah Manolakos, Grade 3
Public School 131, NY

Autumn

A pples are yummy and tasty when you put caramel on them
U mbrellas are wonderful for when the leaves fall
T hanksgiving is a good holiday for a get together
U ncover the turkey mommy, I want to see it
M other can we start the feast now with the family?
N ovember is fun because of Fall and Thanksgiving

Gianna Caminero, Grade 3
Central Park Elementary School, FL

Campfires

Hot, red, flames of fire
Marshmallows, chocolate, and graham crackers
Roasting, laughing, and talking
Time going by
Feels like it's just begun, but it's been 2 hours and it's done.

Erin Kilkenny, Grade 3
Center School, MA

High Merit Poems – Grades K, 1, 2, and 3

Garland
G arland is a decoration.
A ny name that is Garland could be a last name.
R arely people's last name is Garland.
L ike my last name Garland?
A rlene Garland is my Grandma.
N atalie's last name is Garland.
D addy was the first person in my family to have the last name Garland.

Elizabeth Garland, Grade 1
St Stephen's School, NY

I Can Promote Peace by
Sharing:
Telling everyone to be kind and friendly
To spread love all over the earth
To reuse, reduce and recycle to keep the earth healthy
To not litter, but to pick up the litter
To plant trees and flowers
And, to make things out of old things.

Alexa Poupis, Grade 2
Our Lady of Mercy Regional School, NY

Penguin
P enguins have babies called chicks
E ggs get warm under their father
N eeds down fur to survive the cold weather
G etting food for the babies is the mom's job
U nusual how the mother spits up food for babies to eat
I t is freezing in Antarctica, the home of penguins.
N ervous that mom won't come back with food.

Grace Bauder, Grade 3
McKinley Elementary School, PA

How I Promote Peace
Peace is a wonderful thing. I like it so much I want to sing!
When I feel peace, it meets my gaze, everyone uses peace in their days.
How I promote peace, okay I will say it, if you really must know. I will stay back and wait for someone who's slow.
Well, there are more ways you can show peace.
By helping someone, cheer a friend up when they are sad, make someone laugh make them feel glad.

Katie Marie Bohner, Grade 3
Our Lady of Mercy Regional School, NY

Halloween Night

One Halloween I had such a fright,
when my friends and I saw a scary sight.
Johnny, Cameron and Christopher were there,
when a ghost jumped out and gave us a scare.

We saw goblins and ghouls and things in the dark,
we started to run when we heard a dog bark.
My friends screamed and shouted and acted like fools,
when around the corner came 3 more ghouls.

We ran and we ran up and down the street,
then a monster grabbed Johnny by his two feet.
Christopher and Cameron thought they were fine,
when out of the brushes came Frankenstein.

More monsters came and I thought I was dead,
then I suddenly woke up and fell out of bed.
I was happy and glad there was no more fear,
then I realized it will all start again next year.

Blake Camerlin, Grade 3
St Alexis School, PA

The Cute Duck Named Chuck

On the farm there is a very lucky duck
And his cute name is Chuck
He likes to play with his soccer ball
Rolling it down one great big hall
In the barn, he watches the brown and white horse
Go round and round the giant course
Then he visits the chickens' pen
But he better watch out for the cranky hen
Next he plays with the pigs
That's strange, they are all wearing wigs
And last he visits the big brown cows
But they are all asleep now
Chuck is suddenly tired, so he goes to bed
And lays down his tiny yellow head
But he can't sleep
So he counts some sheep
And slowly he falls fast asleep
Good night Chuck the duck

Julia James, Grade 2
Infant Jesus School, NH

High Merit Poems – Grades K, 1, 2, and 3

Home for Christmas

When it's cold and snowy,
I'll be at home for Christmas,
To hear the family scream with joy and happiness,
To look at the decorations on the Christmas tree,
While I sleep and wait for Santa,
Christmas will be back again next year,
And I'll be waiting for Santa.

Astrid Dimas, Grade 3
Marie Curie Institute, NY

My Pup Cookie

I cared for and loved my dog Cookie,
He was hit by a truck and died when he jumped out the window.
It was sad; he was my favorite pup ever.
Cookie did tricks for me and everything,
Then he died…
I was sad
So sad.

Roberto Ramos, Grade 2
New York Institute for Special Education, NY

Snowmen

S parkling like diamonds
N ever sit on it
O n the shimmering white earth
W ish it would never melt
M any children make them
E very one needs a nose
N o buttons — so use raisins!

Ashley Oberlin, Grade 3
George Hersey Robertson Intermediate School, CT

Penguin

P enguin fathers stay with the egg
E mperor penguins eat fish
N o nests are made for their eggs
G enerous amount of food given by mother
U nderwater looking for food
I s very familiar with living in cold conditions
N ot able to live in hot weather

Allison Brubaker, Grade 3
McKinley Elementary School, PA

Giuliana

Giuliana
Funny, pretty, loving, cuddly
Daughter of Maria and Angelo
Sister of Gabriella
Loves mommy, daddy, nonna
Who likes makeup, jewelry, *Monsters Inc.*
Who hates homework, chores
Who would like to go to The Outer Banks, Disney and Washington
Resident of Grand Island
Congi

Giuliana Congi, Grade 2
St Stephen's School, NY

Black Cats

B lack spooky cats
L ooking for something to eat.
A nxious cats want to share their food with their family.
C ats' fur is pitch black.
K eeping their family warm.

C ats have glowing eyes in the dark.
A ngry meowing!
T errifying!
S pooky!!!

Alexis Graziano, Grade 2
Consolidated School, CT

Chipmunks

C hipmunks scurry around the woods trying to find some nuts.
H urry chipmunks; try and find some nuts fast. Winter's coming up!
I see some chipmunks running wild around the rock wall in the warm autumn sun.
P erching in their tree crunching and
M unching on nuts mmmmmmmmmmmmm yummy nuts!!!!!!!!!!!
U ntil a fox comes. STAY IN YOUR TREE!!
N ice and safe in their tree, the fox runs away. They
K eep trying and trying to finish their tree hole.
S o now they can be nice and warm and ready for winter.

Sammi Ruggiero, Grade 2
Consolidated School, CT

Gingerbread Cookies

The cookies wait by the Christmas tree for Santa Claus.
Gingerbread cookies taste gingery and remind me of Christmas.
They taste the best when they just come out of the oven.
I hope Santa saves me some cookies on Christmas day.

Bradley Depew, Grade 3
Riverton Public School, NJ

Dogs

Dogs are barking, eating and running.
Children like looking, running and feeding dogs.
We are having fun with dogs.

Kevin McGarvey, Grade 3
Our Lady of Hope School, NY

Outside

A bird is flying
It is beautiful outside
Trees are growing tall

Benjamin Holcman, Grade 2
Virginia A Boone Highland Oaks Elementary School, FL

The Waterfall

Water is pretty
Its sound is so rough and tough
And rocks surround it…

Gabriel Isaac Feldenkrais, Grade 2
Virginia A Boone Highland Oaks Elementary School, FL

The Sun

The water is warm.
The sun is hot and shining
The benches are nice.

Luke Rier, Grade 2
Virginia A Boone Highland Oaks Elementary School, FL

Nature

Water is pretty
As much as a flower is
And so are roses

Christina Maineri, Grade 2
Virginia A Boone Highland Oaks Elementary School, FL

Animals Aren't Cannibals

School is cool so I'm not a fool.
And to an animal I can't be cruel.

A male whale doesn't have one scale.
But he has a wonderful tail.

Old black crow, do not go slow
Or you will surely hurt your toe.

A fox does not live in a box
And he can't get chicken pox.

A tiger eats meat and he has four feet,
But his fur gives him too much heat.

An X-rayed fish does not make a good dish,
And not to eat one is my wish.

Drinking eggnog in the fog,
I lost my dog under a log,

A kangaroo, which I named Pooh,
Lives in a zoo with nothing to do.

A ladybug hides under a rug.
That's better than in my mug.

Since my collection's not finished yet,
I'm thinking of animals I still haven't met.

Samuel Master, Grade 1
The American Academy, PA

Christmas Visitor

Ho, Ho, Ho!
Who do you know?
I think I see someone
With a big red coat
A long white beard
A huge red sack
And he seems to like cookies!
Ho, Ho, Ho!

Julia Casella, Grade 2
Worthington Hooker School – K-2 Campus, CT

High Merit Poems – Grades K, 1, 2, and 3

Autumn
Autumn
A pples and acorns
U nderground tunnels
T urning leaves
U mbrellas wet
M isty and mulchy
N uts all collected
Autumn

Adarsh Varghese, Grade 2
Worthington Hooker School – K-2 Campus, CT

Love

Roses are red
Violets are blue
No one is as sweet as you
Your eyes shine in my soul
No one is as nice and sweet as you, know
Love is from my heart, it flows from me to you
I hope you feel the same way I do

Diana Fred, Grade 3
Number 12 Elementary School, NJ

Riding

When I am riding, I feel such a joy.
Having the power and so much glee.
I love when I canter by the green tree.
When I trot, I feel so happy.
When I go over a jump, everyone cheers for me.
My pony is so nice.
Furby, you are the love of my life.

Madison Jones, Grade 3
Sweetwater Episcopal Academy, FL

Holiday

H o Ho Ho — Christmas is the day Jesus was born.
O h what a beautiful heart for Valentine's day.
L ick, lick I can't wait to eat turkey for Thanksgiving
I love New Year's Day.
D ays are magical
A nother magical time is Christmas
Y es — it is that time of year!

Mariandre Lopez, Grade 3
Northeast Elementary School, NY

Squirrel

S campering through my yard it hurried to a nut by a tree.
Q uietly he sat there for about 15 minutes. I looked out the window
U ntil he left. He went fast
I nto the woods. Looking around he finally found a
R abbit right in the back of the woods.
He hurried across the street and he saw a
R abbit with its brother
E ating a germy nut. It was laying on a
L eaf. He chomped on the nut!

Alex Jansen, Grade 2
Consolidated School, CT

Kristen

Friendly, happy, fun, funny
Daughter of Amy and Tom
Sister of Kelly and Riley
Loves dad, mom, sisters
Who likes ice cream, toys, pizza
Who hates peanut butter, Star Wars
Who would like to be rich, get good grades, go to Florida
Resident of Grand Island
Coghlan

Kristen Coghlan, Grade 2
St Stephen's School, NY

Autumn

A pples are in season
U nusual and amazing things happen
T urkeys are yummy
U se gravy on your turkey
M ama helps me make a scarf
N obody can resist my famous pumpkin pie

Valentina Gispert, Grade 3
Central Park Elementary School, FL

Owls

O wls being spooky in the night
W hen it's pitch black out, it's quiet in the night.
L ooking for tasty food in the night sky.
S eeing their food and gobbling food up
1 by 1 until they're full.

Joey Rynkiewicz, Grade 2
Consolidated School, CT

High Merit Poems – Grades K, 1, 2, and 3

Mr. Mike

Mr. Mike!
A funny guy!
He says hello.
He says goodbye.
He always calls me
By my name.
Mr. Mike!

Roxanne Kelly, Grade 2
Worthington Hooker School – K-2 Campus, CT

Waves

The waves at the beach are big and strong.
The waves at the beach are rough and blue.
I tried to swim in the water but the strong waves wouldn't allow me to.

The waves at the beach are big and strong.
People try to go in but the strong waves kick them out.
The waves at the beach are super strong.

Jaslyn Caraballo, Grade 3
Public School 131, NY

Submarine

Fast as a jet.
Strong as a bull.
Sneaky as a fox.
Black as night.
You'll know when it's there,
When your eyes occur to a strange black thing in the water.

Bryan Nam, Grade 2
Corl Street Elementary School, PA

My Life as a Pilgrim

If I was a Pilgrim I would cook, and sew all day.
I would play shooting marbles with my sisters.
My family and I would eat seafood with duck.
My dad would hunt duck all day.
My mom and I would cook the ducks for the side dish.
My favorite chore would be sewing clothes.

Alyssa Ednie, Grade 3
St Mary School, NY

Halloween

On a dark night called Halloween
Green skeletons walk around me
See the ghosts walking around the headstones that say "R.I.P."
Straps with gooey blood
Mud on the ghost's face
It vanishes without a trace
Halloween is quite a night!

Shelley Pleva, Grade 2
Wellington School, FL

Bronx Zoo

When I'm in the mood to see animals,
I'll be visiting the Bronx Zoo,
To see the gorillas and the lions,
To watch people eat Dippin' Dots and pizza,
While I walk through the zoo,
I'll be back again next June,
When I'm in the mood to see animals.

Jordan Borreli, Grade 3
Marie Curie Institute, NY

Football Protection

Fun playing on the football field
Snap the ball, on the go, hitting the person in front of me
I'm the best running back
Awesome game
Like it!
Lots of teammates
Lots of fun!

Elijah Rojas, Grade 2
Carlyle C Ring Elementary School, NY

Domino's Pizza

When I'm in the mood for pizza,
I'll be eating at Domino's Pizza,
To hear the yelling kids and the music playing,
To watch kids eating and people laughing,
While I sit in my seat and wait for my pizza,
I'll be back again next Friday,
When I'm in the mood for pizza.

Angelica Rivera, Grade 3
Marie Curie Institute, NY

Fall

Fall is here.
And an ant is crawling in your plate.
Next a red leaf falls from the tree.
And fall is cold.
Sometimes it is hot.
A yellow leaf falls too.
And every leaf falls from the tree.
And if winter comes everything will be white.
I like fall.

Brian Liu, Grade 1
Children's Village, PA

The Owl

At night's darkest hour when everyone is sleeping,
where the vines and twigs hang together,
the owl glides silently through the sky
finding food for her precious babies.
She searches all night swooping and diving
through the chill of the night air.
And as dawn marches over the land,
her family is fed and sleeping.

Ben Short, Grade 3
Farmingville Elementary School, CT

Autumn

A pples are good but to make them better, add caramel
U seful ingredients are pumpkins, but to make them good, add cinnamon
T hanksgiving day is very good, but to make it better you add pumpkin pie
U nder the oak tree, the leaves turn yellow, red, and orange
M y mom makes sweet potatoes with cinnamon
N obody in my family will eat pumpkin pie because it is all mine!

Joseph Castillo, Grade 3
Central Park Elementary School, FL

Horses

Horses are nice.
Oh how I love them.
They could be brown, white or black.
I had one I called Snow White because she is white.

Nydia Clifton, Grade 2
Sweetwater Episcopal Academy, FL

The Dream Sleepover
It was a full moon night.
Oh hush, it's time to go to bed.
A pillow burst like a volcano,
Because the girls wanted to have fun.
Can I call my mommy?
Lips of black
The moon awaits me.
Quietness takes over the air.
Sleep tight.
Megan Sweeney, Grade 3
Oak Ridge Elementary School, PA

Fall
Fall is coming.
Me and my sister and
My friend are going to
See the colorful leaves.
The wind is blowing.
The leaves are going
to be red, yellow,
brown and orange.
Sharon Wu, Grade 2
Children's Village, PA

Fall Is Coming
Fall is coming
The wind blowing
Get some treats
And have some fun
My friend is coming
To get some treats
My favorite day is
Halloween
Kathleen Chen, Grade 1
Children's Village, PA

Snow
S ometimes there is a lot.
N ever in the summer.
O nly in the winter.
W hen will it come?
Nick Esposito, Grade 2
St John the Apostle Catholic School, VA

My First Trip to Disney
D awn awaits…get up!
I t's time! Drive! Drive!
S wan Hotel — here we come!!!
N eat, huh? Yup, sure is!
E arly afternoon we got there!
Y eah!! We get to go to an arcade!

W ow! This room rocks!!
O kay, after we shop, we eat!!
R oller coasters are
L ots and lots of fun!!
D rive! Drive! Home — here we come!!!
Joey Walker, Grade 3
Robeson Elementary School, PA

My Pop-Pop
We play football together
Watch AMC on TV
We go to the Dollar Store
We buy 3 bags of chips
and Pop-Pop gets 2 packs
of crackers.
We go back home
I take out the crackers
I eat 2 bags of chips
Save the last bag
eat it
after dinner
Jaden Smith, Grade 3
William M Meredith School, PA

Christmas
C hristmas trees are beautiful
H olidays are nice
R eindeer in the sky with Santa
I nteresting presents
S anta Claus
T aking Christmas wrapping off presents
M y gifts are cool
A present from Santa Claus
S nowmen are cool
Jennifer Argueta, Grade 3
Bensley Elementary School, VA

Grandmom
Pretty, nice
Loving, helping, cooking
She will always love me
Mama
Abby Shapiro, Grade 2
William M Meredith School, PA

Birthday
Fun, surprise
Surprising, exciting, helping
Everyone gives you a present
Happy Birthday
Morgan Bryson, Grade 2
William M Meredith School, PA

Bees
B ees sting
E ach one makes honey
E at nectar
S tripes of black and yellow
Preston Stride, Grade 2
Marie Curie Institute, NY

Summer Days
Summer days!
The sun is hot.
The water is warm.
The breeze will cool you down.
Summer days!
Catalina Homann, Grade 2
Worthington Hooker School – K-2 Campus, CT

A New Journey
The raindrops float to the lake
Like feathers
So softly
They start a new journey in the lake.
Ryan Oberg, Grade 2
Carlyle C Ring Elementary School, NY

The Rainy Day
Hazy gray
Foggy, rainy day
Someone fishing all alone
Red and yellow leaves blowing around.
Landon Blood, Grade 2
Carlyle C Ring Elementary School, NY

Index

Abad, Jeffrey 67
Abbott, Alexis 39
Abeles, Olivia 123
Aberdeen, Korey 103
Acharya, Iman 30
Acosta, Faith 123
Acosta, Jeremiah 42
Adams, Mia 129
Adams, Samantha 52
Agene, Enyojo 27
Aleong, Romelo 131
Allen, Joshua 98
Allen, Soledad 86
Allison, Alexander 110
Alston, Ra'Nayah 137
Alvarez, Christie 34
Alvarez, Enrique 136
Alverio, Anthony 21
Amato, Carly 19
Amenda, Cydney 73
Anderson, Quinton 113
Anger, Sam 135
Ardila, Marcos 23
Argiro, Emma 134
Argueta, Jennifer 150
Ariker, Levi 104
Armer, Austin 42
Armstrong, Cade 123
Arndt, Michael 77
Arzu, Trinity 37
Asel, Raeann 31
Auble, Ashlynn 124
Azzi, Sara 88
Bagdy, Harsh 90
Baker, Kole 29
Balgobin, Isabella 25
Ball, Meagan 100
Bankuti, Connor 46
Barbieri, Ralph 94
Barker, Brooke 44

Barnecott, Trent 32
Barnes, Elijah 60
Barr, Desiree 74
Bartlo, Anna 91
Bauder, Grace 139
Begum, Amena 133
Behar, Robert 123
Bell, Abby 23
Berchtold, Sam 23
Berlinger, Connor 105
Berrocal, Adam 73
Berry, Brooke 33
Besse, Makenzie 36
Best, Cole 26
Bifulco, Harry 120
Biondo, Jessie 63
Birch, Abigail 84
Bissoondial, Ethan 58
Bixby, Carter 37
Blood, Landon 151
Bloom, Damon 14
Boccasino, Nicholas 129
Bohner, Katie Marie 139
Bokina, Angelina 112
Bond, Ashley 124
Bond, Georgia 92
Borra, Kavya 103
Borreli, Jordan 148
Bottisti, Kyle 25
Bowers, Griffin 32
Bowman, Sierra 59
Boyczuk, Meghan 79
Bradley, Owen 93
Bradshaw, Damon 124
Brand, Andrew 114
Braunschweig, Zev 22
Brave, Angela 43
Brice, D'Angelo 127
Brodowski, Thomas 61
Broides, Daniel 19

Brown, Alyson 13
Brown, Clayton 99
Brown, Dillon 130
Brown, Sydney 88
Brown, Taylor 48
Brown, Zack 108
Brubaker, Allison 141
Bryson, Morgan 151
Buck, Andrew 58
Buffaloe, A'Mair 21
Bugayer, Chaim 22
Buhl, Rachael 102
Bungatavula, Yajat 79
Buonanno, Alexandra 21
Burba, Carlyn 65
Burgos, Sara 114
Burner, Mary 87
Byerly, Dylan 111
Caggiano, Cameron 22
Cagnassola, John 107
Calabrese, Natalie 97
Camerlin, Blake 140
Caminero, Gianna 138
Campbell, Deanna 103
Campbell, Jordan 136
Campbell, Joseph 114
Capofreddi, Emily 39
Capuano, Emma Lauryn 32
Caraballo, Jaslyn 147
Carl, Evan 137
Carl, Mitchell 58
Casella, Julia 144
Cassarrubias, Armando .. 97
Cassidy, Dylan 45
Cassille, Anthony 86
Castillo, Joseph 149
Castor, Michael 48
Castor, Wren 58
Cavalieri, Brianna 42
Cheek, Mariah 76

A Celebration of Poets – East Grades K-3 Fall 2010

Chen, Kathleen 150	D'Amore, Nicholas 136	Feikls, Mason 31
Chevalier, Elyssa 87	D'Angelo, Sal................... 59	Feldenkrais,
Chifa, Valentina 96	DaGraca, Isaac............... 127	Gabriel Isaac............ 143
Chimelis, Nicholas 109	Daley, Scott...................... 35	Ferriera, Jayden............... 13
Chiodi, Gianluca.............. 59	Darden, Shadia 25	Ferriso, Josephine 117
Chisek, Zachary 78	Darpino, Anthony 46	Ficarra, Benjamin........... 27
Chou, Riley...................... 95	David, Nuriel................... 26	Fierro, Sabrina............... 129
Clark, Tre' 101	Dawson, Jacob................. 22	Fiet, Jake.......................... 92
Clifton, Nydia................ 149	Dell, Angela................... 102	Figueroa, Justina 13
Cobarrubia, Benjamin.. 118	DelMonico, Emerson 93	Fillion, Cameron............ 128
Coghlan, Kristen 146	DelValle, Joshua 36	Finello, Jacob R............... 34
Cohen, Preston................. 91	DeNardo, Jane 51	Finn, Michael.................. 60
Collentine, Kassidy........ 113	Depew, Bradley.............. 143	Fischer, Caroline 12
Collins, Rowan 71	DeRosa, Francesca 136	Flaute, Samantha 52
Colon, Nikolett................ 62	Derzavich, Melissa 131	Flood, Christopher 106
Colucci, Sarah Kate 29	DeWitt, Madeleine........... 39	Flora, Abiona................... 29
Comrie, Parris Jade......... 41	DeWitt, Seth 75	Flores, Cynthia................ 16
Conaboy, Alexandra 43	Dias, Mackenzie 47	Flores, Jasmine................ 71
Congi, Giuliana.............. 142	Diehl, Zachary 25	Foster, Olivia 83
Conmy, Kimberly........... 112	DiMaggio, Krista 126	Fred, Diana 145
Conway, Jullianna.......... 108	Dimas, Astrid................. 141	Frew, Daniel 18
Conyers, Brionna 118	Doherty, Isabella............ 132	Freyesien, R.J.................. 120
Conyers, Christopher 55	Donnelly, Emma 113	Friel, Emily.................... 125
Cook, Samuel................... 26	Dooley, Nick 86	Friesen, Colton 57
Cornelson, Holly 36	Dougherty, Kevin............. 52	Gagne, Ashton................. 39
Corrado, Danielle............ 90	Drake, Julian.................... 65	Gaines, Carson 68
Correa, Daryel................. 24	Dreyer, Isabella 16	Galan, Carlos 19
Cortez, Adriana 120	Drobnak, Amanda............ 88	Gallagher, Matthew....... 113
Costanzo, Ana 95	Drown, Nicholas 87	Gallo, Emilio................. 114
Cotton, Aaliyah 62	Duma, Brock................. 112	Garcia, Amaya............... 130
Courduff, Brian................ 71	Duma, Hailey 62	Garland, Elizabeth........ 139
Courduff, Ceili'-Ann........ 73	Duong, Eric 73	Gaskin II, Damiane 132
Courtmanche, Tatum 43	Duran, Trinity.................. 87	Gelman, Alex................... 49
Creelman, Marissa........... 94	Durinick, CJ..................... 94	Geoghegan, Natalie 72
Crisp, Logan 132	Ebeling, Blake.................. 82	Geras, Alexis................. 108
Crowe, Renée................... 63	Ednie, Alyssa 147	Gervais,
Crownover, Jesse.............. 65	Eppinger, Derek............. 126	Kaitlin Elizabeth........ 29
Cruz, Dylinn.................... 61	Esposito, Matthew 38	Gesimondo, Gianna...... 108
Cruz, Leah....................... 66	Esposito, Nick................ 150	Gewirtz, Menachem........ 26
Cubarrubia, Blake 91	Estrada, Ethan 61	Giannopoulos, Amanda.. 93
Cunningham, Camille.. 110	Fabiyan, David 63	Gilgar, Adrianna 127
Curran, Matthew............. 76	Falbo, Samantha 113	Giraldo, Eric.................... 44
Cybulka, Julia 111	Farley, Paige 26	Gispert, Valentina 146
Cyr, Jaslyn....................... 91	Faye, Natalie.................. 125	Goar, May 23
D., Justin.......................... 88	Fechter, Aidan 74	Gomes, Michael 18
D'Alessandro, Gianna 72	Fedus, Sophia................... 43	Gomez, Ilyus 66

Index

Gómez, Emma 53	Hinds, Hannah 33	Kelley, Morgan 134
Gongloff, Ana 65	Hoch, Dalton 75	Kelly, Roxanne 147
Gonzalez, Jason 74	Hoffman, Julia 32	Kendra, James 82
Gonzalez, Lasha 71	Holcman, Benjamin 143	Kilburg, Daniel 135
Good, Kortney 130	Hollick, Shannon 15	Kilby, Ryan 73
Gordon, David 22	Homann, Catalina 151	Kilkenny, Erin 138
Gordon-Jones, Jaquant ... 87	Horowitz, Nina 123	Kilmartin, Maddison 129
Gravagna, Julia 63	Hosking, Sarah 85	Kirkland, Benjamin 127
Gray, Ashley 33	Houghwot, Kyler 36	Kirwin, Anna 20
Gray, Chrysta 63	Howard, Brooke 97	Kirwin, Grace 126
Gray, Gabriella 76	Howe, Zackary 33	Kleiner, Livia 120
Graziano, Alexis 142	Hudak, Fisher 117	Klessel, Quinn 19
Graziano, Carisa 44	Huebner, Nadia 65	Klingman, Grace 74
Greenspan, Gabriel 57	Hummer, Aaron 120	Klontz, Ivana 61
Gregory, Jaylen 121	Hurtado, Kelsey 54	Knights, Brandon 106
Greville, Chad 130	Hutchins, Ryan 89	Knisely-Durham, Emily .. 74
Guenoun, Joseph 106	Huyck, Taylor 117	Knox, Maggie 65
Gullifer, Hannah 31	Iacono, Alexander 34	Koehler, Jacob 76
Guneren, Ilayda 73	Inesti, Crystal 88	Koivu, Erik 80
Gural, Thomas 125	Iracheta, Rebecca 80	Koreyva, Ivy 22
Guzman, Felix 48	Izzo, Juliana 44	Kramer, Amelia 31
Habeck, Anthony 126	Jackson, Dana 60	Krishnamoorthy,
Hagan, Connor 36	Jacobowitz, Yaacov 26	Prasanna 12
Haghnejad, Sammy 91	Jacobs, Jennette 131	Kroll, Amanda 90
Halas, Tyler 57	James, Bryanna 87	Krouch, Malone 83
Hallberg, Victoria 31	James, Julia 140	Kulikova, Anna 124
Hammond, Janine 41	James, Kiaya 75	Kulikowski, Maya 48
Hanline, Katie 72	James, Kyla 77	Kurtz, Nick 45
Hans, Philip 88	Jansen, Alex 146	Kussman, Matthew 76
Harnish, Susanna 70	Javage, Toby 94	Ladhani, Sara 80
Harper, William 126	Jimenez, Viviana 116	Lake, Jacob 53
Harris, Kiyah 63	Johnpoll, Malachai 121	Lamb, Sean 115
Harris, Leah 97	Johnson, Almasi 78	Lampognana, Laura 67
Harris, Vida 23	Johnson, Heidi 58	Lamsal, Siddhartha 129
Harrison, Alana 126	Jones, Elijah 33	Langille, Abigail 102
Haught, Ansley 35	Jones, Madison 145	Langley, Kaylah 15
Hayer, Sam 50	Jones, Myeeka 109	Lare, Lannen 82
Haynes, Camden Scout . 122	Kaatz, Christopher M. 64	Laundau, Chaim 22
Healey, Nicole 116	Kabongo, Mbiya 127	Lawless, Abigail 72
Henry, Zoe 99	Kaelin, Jessica 91	Le, Lang 83
Henry Pabon, Jordan 53	Kapusi, Victoria 100	Lee, Jada 132
Herrera, Moises 59	Karnes, Hope 49	Lee, Karina 117
Herrera, Shanelle 94	Katella, Katie 107	Lee, Tyler 50
Heske, Zachary 81	Kearney, Yosi 81	Lehr, Kaitlynn 96
Heywood, Emma 97	Kehoe, Courtney 20	Lemoine, Mary 124
Hickman, Kathryn 33	Kelley, Isabella 108	Leon, Bibiana 126

A Celebration of Poets – East Grades K-3 Fall 2010

Levitan, Amani............... 112
Levya, Kelin 80
Lewis, Azaria 113
Li, Alan 73
Li, Maggie........................ 29
Lieberman, Rachel.......... 47
Lim, Serena 96
Limey, Perrin................. 114
Lin, Samantha 61
Lister, Madison 130
Liu, Brian 149
Liu, Jiaming 14
Lombard, Anthony 115
Lopez, Ehunixe 87
Lopez, Mariandre 145
Lovegren, Jacquelynn 81
Lowe, Jacob 74
Lubowiecki, Phillip....... 119
Lucas, Jordyn 51
Luna, Brian 54
MacDonald, Elias 119
MacDonough, Joseph...... 63
Maddonni, Brianna 93
Mader, Jonathan 79
Madigan, Brynn 128
Madigan, Riley 84
Magner, Sean 51
Mahon, Ally 26
Maineri, Christina 143
Major, Rachael................ 51
Maksimovich, Owen........ 50
Maldonado, Samuel......... 96
Malec, Victoria 128
Malik, Hurayrah 110
Malik, Rayyan 91
Malishewsky, Maya.......... 24
Maltin, Dylan 128
Malvita, Ashli 81
Mangelli, Victoria 35
Manolakos, Savannah .. 138
Marcellus, Christina 60
Marinov, Alinah 74
Marrero, Ashley............... 32
Marshall, Emma 27
Marti, Aryella 44
Martin, Alexander......... 125

Martin, Amethyst 73
Martin, Avery................. 128
Martin, Margaret 48
Martinez, Chantze........... 50
Martinez, Laura 94
Martinez, Wilfredo 94
Master, Samuel 144
Mathew, Emil 82
McCain, Christina........... 57
McClanahan, Donavin.... 36
McCloud, Kennedy 86
McCombe, Sarah........... 105
McComsey, Dylan 96
McConnell, Shawn 115
McDonnell, Mairin.......... 71
McGann, Liam 86
McGarvey, Kevin........... 143
McGee, Connor................ 78
McGinnis, Michael........ 119
McGoldrick, Liam 35
McGuinness Getzinger,
 Kyle............................... 73
McKay, Taylor.................. 89
McLaughlin, Gavin 26
Meade, Christopher......... 80
Medrano, Destiny............ 29
Mei, Michael.................... 50
Melchiorre, Nicole........... 58
Melendez, Nevaeh 29
Mello, Jacob..................... 65
Mendez, Naselin 70
Mendiola, Gianna............ 42
Merced, Samuel 96
Meyer, Aelah.................... 47
Meyer, Pisay 130
Miceli, Gio....................... 71
Mikol, Hannah................. 81
Milette, Elisha 48
Millemann, Nikki............. 51
Miller, Brandon............... 53
Miller, Matthew 110
Millington, Abrien.......... 132
Mindell, Aaron 22
Mistriner, Marissa 81
Mitchell, Austin............. 128
Mitchell, Cameron 91

Modano, Guido 104
Modzelewski, Dominick.. 89
Moka, Turiya................... 33
Moleski, Nicolette............ 91
Molnarova, Sarah 64
Monsorno, Luke 81
Morris, Dylan 29
Mosca, Gabrielle 46
Moschello, Elizabeth..... 106
Moses, Brett..................... 94
Muiter, Shane.................. 57
Mularczyk, Sebastian...... 99
Muniz, Talisha 112
Muro, Jenna 63
Murphy, Jailyn................. 58
Murphy, Sarah 54
Muschette, Ansel 98
Myers, Emily 83
Myers, Hannah................ 52
Nam, Bryan.................... 147
Nam, Yongjae................... 22
Naples, Mike.................... 23
Naugles, Matthew W........ 80
Neciunas-Atwell, Mya...... 86
Nelson, Nicky 51
Newton, Karen 24
Ngo, Steven 53
Nieto, Anayeli 26
Nieves, Emilio 120
Nieves, Mia 62
Nirschl, Mollie................. 44
Nodes, Amber Leigh 51
Noe, Jonathan 71
Novobilsky, Kevin 44
Novosel, Lexi 31
Null, Laura...................... 55
Nunnally, Lexi 66
Nycz, Olivia 126
Nygaard, Alyssa 96
O'Brien, Joseph 119
O'Donnell, Aeven 102
O'Donnell, Caroline........ 60
O'Hara, Ian 114
O'Rourke, Dominic.......... 82
O'Shaughnessy, Claire .. 104
O'Sullivan, Kelsey 112

Page 156

Index

Oakes, Alyssa 31
Oberg, Ryan 151
Oberlin, Ashley 141
Odzer, Michael 122
Oehler, Terrance 16
Olivo, Nathaly 132
Olokungbemi, Toun 127
Ordas, Anika 114
Ortiz, Jorge 32
Osegueda Ramos, Elvira. 59
Osit, Lindsey 124
Ovack, Emily 130
Ovack, Marissa 102
Paguirigan, Justin 78
Pam, Avrohom Yaakov 26
Panepinto, Emmanuela . 63
Parker, Brenden 54
Paxson, Ava 56
Pedersen, Margo 121
Pedre, Jessie 26
Pelloni, Jackie 28
Pepin, Luke 66
Perez, Alejandra 107
Perez, Danixi 116
Perillo, Elizabeth 64
Perlman, Autumn 49
Perlman, Julie 56
Pertab, Gabriella 104
Phillip, India 122
Phillips, Olivia 58
Phillips, Ryan 108
Pickering, William 82
Pinand, Brian 127
Pinciaro, Olivia 50
Pira, Nicholas 96
Piskorowski, Marty 59
Pleva, Shelley 148
Plewinski, Abigail 21
Poupis, Alexa 139
Poupis, Kameron 71
Powell, Aristotle 37
Preble, Elliott 87
Preston, Julia 78
Proctor, Ainsley 62
Profit, David 101
Purohit, Rishi 46

Quartararo, Caleb 95
Ramella, Victoria 74
Ramos, Roberto 141
Ramos, Vanessa Guadalupe .. 118
Randig, Sarah 39
Ravichandren, Abinaya 117
Reed, Michael 102
Reyes, Katherine 121
Rier, Luke 143
Riga, Gregorio 59
Riggs, Kelly 86
Rivas, Brennen 129
Rivera, Angelica 148
Rivera, Destiny 76
Rivera, Kayla 48
Rivera, Matthew 113
Rivera, Selena 34
Rizzo, Jack 20
Roberts, Tiffani 43
Robic, Kayleigh 133
Robie, Jessie 79
Robinson, Samuel 37
Rodecker, Nick 136
Rodriguez, Brendan 59
Rodriguez, David 21
Rodriguez Garcia, Cindy. 17
Rogowski, Karina 113
Rojas, Elijah 148
Roman, Angelica 136
Roman, Madison 62
Romero, David 39
Romero, George 88
Rosenbaum, Emma 30
Ross, Elizabeth 69
Rothman, Kaia 129
Rowland, Dillon 120
Rozance, Dominic 107
Ruggiero, Christine 94
Ruggiero, Sammi 142
Rumberger, Allie 105
Rupp-Coppi, Leo 17
Rust, Paulina 46
Rynkiewicz, Joey 146
Saburova, Yekaterina 54
Sacco, Sydney 127

Saf, Ainsley 31
Salcedo, Alize 89
Salvacion, Sydney Rizalinda A. ... 97
Samolyuk, Gabriel 79
Sanchez, Daniel 89
Santana, Victoria 29
Santiago, Jiarmani 49
Santiago, Vanessa 76
Santos, Christopher 19
Saravia, Barbara 91
Saro, Adora 56
Scandrett, Mia 36
Scerbak, Dominique Gabrielle . 70
Schifferdecker, Grace 59
Schneider, Mia 114
Schneider, Michael 69
Schnorbus, Taylor 54
Schoenhardt, Antonio 34
Schreck, Ephraim 22
Schuckman, Avi 51
Scott, Jada 86
Seeley, Alanis 43
Serttas, Madison 16
Sevor, Kelly 32
Shapiro, Abby 151
Shaw, Matthew 44
Shek, Jonathan 85
Shenkman, Davis 137
Sheppard, Cora 34
Sherry, Jordyn 15
Shewchuk, Catherine 101
Short, Ben 149
Shrubb, Mackenzie 31
Silva, Benny 81
Simko, Megan 62
Simmons, Cole 79
Sinton, Nicole 26
Sisson, Tyler 108
Skinner, Tiara 37
Skipper, Sara 76
Sklar, Nachi 51
Slaton, Jarrett 47
Slezak, Logan 32
Slovack, Alex 76

Smith, Ayana 48	Voutsinos, Matthew 56
Smith, Brennan 114	Vrooman, Laurel 48
Smith, Jaden 150	Walker, Joey 150
Smith, Josie 32	Walls, Kai 62
Somridhivej, Marwynn . 111	Walters, Joey 130
Spady, Desmond 102	Wang, Jessica 124
Spady, Destiny 46	Washington, Amya 138
Spinelli, Caleb 59	Wasserman, Franklin 101
Stenzel, David 115	Welton, Lexi 18
Storm, Ashya 137	Wheeler, Gabriel 74
Storti, Frankie 92	White, Alexa 43
Strickland, Athena 129	Wiethorn, Joseph 40
Stride, Preston 151	Wightman, Evan 14
Stripeikis, Abigail 106	Wilson, Zachary 81
Suber, Justin 130	Winegrad, Myles 82
Swanson, Danielle 31	Winn, Cecelia 28
Sweeney, Megan 150	Wolberg, David 22
Synor, Emilee 45	Wolff, Jonathan 50
Szabo, Kylee 32	Wrobel, Ethan 90
Szabo, Ryan 28	Wu, Sharon 150
Szymanski, Thomas 89	Wurster, Megan 65
Taborda, Sebastian 50	Yanez, Brandon 68
Tattersall, Riley 40	Yarka, Julianna 81
Taylor, Ezra 108	Yuen, Matthew 74
Taylor, Sapphire 46	Zabel, Kyle 27
Thai, Brian 35	Zabielski, Zowie 76
Thompson, Reese 97	Zarwin, Michael 136
Tomlinson, Avery 131	Zeng, Ivan 36
Torres, Julissa 29	Zhang, Steven 116
Torres, Luzmari 63	Zhao, Junhao 34
Trastsianka, Daniel 111	Zinser, Amanda 52
Troche, Karen 89	Zucker, Jacob 20
Troutman, Lason 46	
Uriguen, Cameron 127	
Vadodaria, Raj 83	
Valentin, Japhet 120	
Valenzuela, Amanda 88	
Vallo, Olivia 22	
Varghese, Abel 44	
Varghese, Adarsh 145	
Vaught, Addison 97	
Vest, Grace 68	
Vilela-Ortiz, Keisha 38	
Vincent, Ethan 136	
Violette, Katherine 34	
Voege, Samantha 47	

Author Autograph Page

Author Autograph Page